By Devon Kade
and The Sum It Collective

CHRISTIANITY
Summarized

A Complete Guide to the History, Beliefs, and Practices of the Christian Faith

West Agora Int

West Agora Int
Timisoara 2025
WEST AGORA INT S.R.L.
All Rights Reserved
Copyright © WEST AGORA INT 2025

CHRISTIANITY Summarized
Copyright © 2025
West Agora Int

All rights reserved. No part of this book may be copied, reproduced, distributed, or transmitted in any form or by any means, including photocopying, recording, or other electronic or mechanical methods, without prior written permission from the publisher, except in the case of brief quotations used in a review, article, or scholarly critique.

This book is intended as a general resource and does not constitute professional advice. While every effort has been made to ensure the accuracy and completeness of the information contained herein, the author and publisher disclaim any liability or responsibility for errors, omissions, or outcomes arising from the use of this material.

Requests for permission or inquiries regarding this work may be directed to the publisher:

West Agora Int

All trademarks and registered trademarks appearing in this book are the property of their respective owners. Their inclusion does not imply any affiliation or endorsement by them.

Unauthorized reproduction or distribution of this book is strictly prohibited and may result in civil and criminal penalties under applicable copyright laws.

Published by West Agora Int
Edited by West Agora Int
Cover Art by West Agora Int

The Ultimate Guide to the World's Most Influential Faith

For over two thousand years, Christianity has shaped civilizations, inspired revolutions, and transformed countless lives. But what is Christianity at its core? What do its followers truly believe? How did it evolve from a small group of disciples to the largest faith in the world?

This book is your **comprehensive, yet accessible** guide to the history, doctrines, and practices of Christianity. From the life of Jesus Christ to the theological debates that divided empires, from ancient traditions to modern-day challenges, Christianity Summarized unveils the depth and complexity of this enduring faith.

Inside, you will discover:
The Foundations of Christianity – Who was Jesus? What is the Trinity? Why is salvation central to the faith?
The Defining Moments – The Great Schism, the Reformation, and the spread of Christianity across the globe.
The Sacred Texts and Teachings – The Old and New Testaments, key doctrines, and the wisdom of great Christian thinkers.
The Practices and Traditions – Worship, sacraments, monastic life, and the role of the Church in society.
The Ongoing Impact – Christianity's relationship with science, politics, and other world religions.
The Future of Christianity – How the faith is evolving in a rapidly changing world.

Whether you are a curious seeker, a lifelong believer, or a scholar looking for a deeper understanding, this book distills the essence of Christianity into an engaging and illuminating read.

A journey through history, theology, and faith awaits. Are you ready to discover Christianity as you've never seen it before?

TABLE OF CONTENTS

Christianity Jargon 6
The Nature and Definition of Christianity 12
The Bible: Old and New Testaments 16
God in Christianity: The Trinity 21
Jesus Christ: His Life and Mission 25
The Crucifixion and Resurrection 30
Salvation and Grace 34
Christian Eschatology: The End Times 39
The Early Church: From Apostles to Councils 44
The Formation of Christian Doctrine 49
The Great Schism: East and West 54
The Protestant Reformation 59
Christianity in the Modern World 64
The Nature of Humanity and Sin 69
The Role of Faith and Works 74
The Church: Its Role and Function 78
Christian Worship and Liturgy 82
Angels, Demons, and the Spiritual Realm 87
Christian Prayer and Devotion 91
Christian Ethics and Morality 96
Christian Festivals and Holy Days 101
Christian Missions and Evangelism 106
Monasticism and Religious Orders 111
Roman Catholicism 116
Eastern Orthodoxy 120
Protestantism and Its Branches 124
Pentecostalism and Charismatic Christianity 129
Non-Trinitarian Christian Movements 134
Christianity and Science 139
Christianity and Politics 144
Christianity and Other Religions 149
Challenges and the Future of Christianity 154
Further Reading 159

 Christianity Jargon

Understanding Christianity requires familiarity with its unique vocabulary, developed over centuries of theological discussion, liturgical practice, and doctrinal evolution. Below is a glossary of Christian terms, designed to help readers grasp key concepts and navigate theological discussions with confidence.

A

Absolution – The formal forgiveness of sins, often given by a priest or minister in the context of confession.

Advent – The liturgical season leading up to Christmas, symbolizing the anticipation of Christ's birth and second coming.

Agnosticism – The belief that the existence of God is unknown or unknowable.

Altar – A sacred table in Christian churches where the Eucharist (Holy Communion) is consecrated.

Amen – A Hebrew word meaning "so be it" or "truly," used at the end of prayers and hymns to express affirmation.

Anathema – A formal condemnation or excommunication issued by the Church against a person or belief deemed heretical.

Angels – Supernatural beings in Christian theology who serve as messengers of God and protectors of humanity.

Apocalypse – A term referring to the end times, derived from the Greek word for "revelation," often associated with the Book of Revelation.

Apostasy – The act of abandoning or renouncing one's Christian faith.

Apostle – One of the twelve disciples chosen by Jesus Christ, as well as later Christian leaders like Paul, tasked with spreading the Gospel.

Apostolic Succession – The belief that Church authority has been passed down in an unbroken line from the apostles through the laying on of hands.

Ascension – The event in which Jesus Christ was taken up to heaven 40 days after His resurrection.

Atonement – The reconciliation between God and humanity through Christ's sacrifice on the cross.

B

Baptism – A sacrament signifying spiritual cleansing, rebirth, and initiation into the Christian faith, performed with water.

Beatitudes – The blessings pronounced by Jesus in the Sermon on the Mount (Matthew 5:3-12), describing the virtues of a godly life.

Benediction – A blessing or prayer given at the conclusion of a worship service.

Bible – The sacred scripture of Christianity, divided into the Old Testament (Hebrew Scriptures) and the New Testament (focused on Jesus Christ).

Blasphemy – Speech or actions showing disrespect toward God or sacred things.

Body of Christ – A term referring both to the physical body of Jesus and the Church as a spiritual community.

Born Again – A phrase describing spiritual rebirth, typically associated with conversion to Christianity.

C

Canon – The official list of books recognized as Scripture in the Bible.

Catechism – A summary of Christian doctrine used for instruction, particularly in preparation for baptism or confirmation.

Charism – A spiritual gift or grace given by the Holy Spirit for the edification of the Church.

Christology – The study of the person, nature, and role of Jesus Christ.

Communion – Also known as the Eucharist or Lord's Supper, a sacrament in which bread and wine symbolize the body and blood of Christ.

Creed – A formal statement of Christian beliefs, such as the Nicene Creed or Apostles' Creed.

Crucifixion – The execution of Jesus Christ on the cross, central to Christian theology of salvation.

Covenant – A solemn agreement between God and His people, such as the Old Covenant with Israel and the New Covenant in Christ.

D

Deacon – A church official responsible for service and administration within the Christian community.

Denomination – A distinct branch or tradition within Christianity, such as Catholicism, Protestantism, or Orthodoxy.

Disciple – A follower of Jesus Christ, particularly the twelve men He personally chose.

Doctrine – Official church teachings on matters of faith and morals.

E

Easter – The most significant Christian holiday, celebrating Jesus' resurrection from the dead.

Ecclesiology – The theological study of the nature and structure of the Church.

Epistle – A letter written by apostles in the New Testament, often addressing early Christian communities.

Eschatology – The study of end times, including topics like the Second Coming, heaven, hell, and the final judgment.

Eucharist – The sacrament of Holy Communion, commemorating Jesus' Last Supper.

Evangelism – The act of spreading the Christian Gospel.

F

Faith – Complete trust in God and His promises, essential to Christian life.

Fellowship – The communal bond among believers in Christ.

Forgiveness – The remission of sins through divine mercy and human reconciliation.

G

Gospel – The "Good News" of Jesus Christ's life, death, and resurrection, also referring to the four biblical accounts written by Matthew, Mark, Luke, and John.

Grace – The unmerited favor and love of God toward humanity.

H

Heaven – The eternal dwelling place of God and the redeemed.

Hell – The place of eternal separation from God, often associated with punishment for sin.

Holy Spirit – The third person of the Trinity, who empowers and sanctifies believers.

I

Incarnation – The Christian belief that Jesus Christ, the Son of God, took on human flesh.

Intercession – Praying on behalf of others.

J

Judgment Day – The future event in which God will judge all humanity.

Justification – The act by which a person is declared righteous before God, often debated as being through faith alone or faith plus works.

K

Kingdom of God – The reign of God in heaven and on earth, as proclaimed by Jesus.

Kyrie Eleison – A Greek phrase meaning "Lord, have mercy," used in Christian prayers and liturgies.

L

Lent – A 40-day period of fasting and repentance before Easter.

Liturgy – The structure and order of Christian worship services.

M

Martyr – A person who dies for their Christian faith.

Messiah – The "Anointed One," referring to Jesus as the fulfillment of Old Testament prophecies.

Missionary – A person who spreads Christianity to different regions of the world.

N

New Testament – The second part of the Christian Bible, focusing on Jesus Christ and the early Church.

Nicene Creed – A fundamental statement of Christian beliefs formulated in 325 AD.

O

Old Testament – The first part of the Christian Bible, containing Jewish scripture and prophecy.

Ordinance – A religious ritual commanded by Christ, such as baptism and communion.

P

Parable – A short story told by Jesus to convey spiritual truths.

Pentecost – The event when the Holy Spirit descended upon the apostles, marking the birth of the Church.

Pope – The leader of the Roman Catholic Church, believed to be the successor of Peter.

R

Redemption – The act of being saved from sin through Christ's sacrifice.

Repentance – Turning away from sin and seeking God's forgiveness.

Resurrection – Jesus' rise from the dead on the third day after His crucifixion.

S

Sacrament – A sacred Christian rite, such as baptism or the Eucharist.

Salvation – The deliverance from sin and its consequences, granted by faith in Jesus Christ.

Sin – Any thought, word, or action that goes against God's will.

T

Trinity – The doctrine that God exists as three persons: Father, Son, and Holy Spirit.

Transubstantiation – The Catholic belief that the bread and wine in the Eucharist become the actual body and blood of Christ.

V-Z

Veneration – The act of showing honor to saints or sacred things.

Vocation – A calling to serve God, often in ministry or religious life.

The Nature and Definition of Christianity

What Christianity is, its essence, and how it differs from other religions.

What is Christianity? On the surface, this seems like a simple question. Most people would say Christianity is a religion that follows Jesus Christ. Some might define it by its holy book, the Bible, or by its moral teachings. Others may see it as a cultural force, shaping Western civilization for over two millennia. And yet, Christianity is far more than just a system of beliefs, a set of rituals, or a historical institution. It is a profound, living tradition that claims to reveal the ultimate nature of reality—who God is, who we are, and what our purpose is in the grand design of existence.

To define Christianity properly, we must first explore its essence—what makes it distinct from all other religious and philosophical systems. Christianity is fundamentally about relationship: the relationship between God and humanity, between the individual and Christ, and between believers as members of the body of Christ. This relational nature sets Christianity apart from many other religious traditions that emphasize laws, rituals, or enlightenment as the primary means of spiritual fulfillment.

But to understand this essence, we must go deeper. We must explore what Christianity believes about God, about humanity, and about the world. We must ask how it compares to other major world religions. And, ultimately, we must understand what it means to call oneself a Christian.

The Core Identity of Christianity

Christianity is, at its heart, a faith centered on Jesus Christ. The name itself reveals this—it is "Christianity" because it is built on Christ.

Christians believe that Jesus was not just a wise teacher, a prophet, or a revolutionary leader, but the Son of God—the divine made flesh. This claim is radical. It means that Christianity is not merely a philosophy (like Stoicism or Confucianism) or a moral code (like legalistic religious traditions), but a revelation of God entering human history in a personal way.

From the very beginning, the Christian faith was not about abstract speculation but about an encounter with a person—Jesus of Nazareth. The first Christians were not merely followers of his teachings; they were witnesses to his life, death, and resurrection. They did not claim merely to believe in his words; they claimed to know him, to have experienced him as alive even after his crucifixion. This personal aspect is crucial because it means that Christianity is not primarily a religion of rules, but of relationship.

This stands in contrast to many other religious traditions. In Hinduism, for example, the ultimate goal is liberation from the cycle of rebirth through enlightenment. In Buddhism, suffering is overcome through detachment and meditation. In Islam, submission to God's will through obedience to the Quran and the Five Pillars is central. Judaism emphasizes a covenantal relationship between God and the Jewish people, expressed through Torah observance.

Christianity, however, claims something unique: God himself has come to humanity in the person of Jesus Christ, and through faith in him, human beings can be reconciled to God not by their own efforts, but by grace.

This idea of grace is another defining feature of Christianity. While many religions teach that human beings must work their way to God—through good deeds, rituals, or enlightenment—Christianity teaches that salvation is a gift from God. This is expressed in Ephesians 2:8-9:

"For by grace you have been saved through faith, and that not of yourselves; it is the gift of God, not of works, lest anyone should boast."

This means that Christianity is not a religion of self-improvement or moral striving alone, but one of divine rescue. Humans, according to Christian teaching, are fallen—incapable of perfect righteousness. But through Jesus, God reaches down to humanity, offering salvation as an act of love.

Christianity's View of God

Another key to understanding Christianity is its unique view of God. Christians believe in one God who exists as three persons—Father, Son, and Holy Spirit. This doctrine, known as the Trinity, is one of Christianity's most defining and mysterious teachings.

Most world religions have either a monotheistic (belief in one God) or polytheistic (belief in many gods) view of divinity. Christianity, while affirming monotheism, also teaches that God exists as a relational being within himself—a divine community of love. This is an idea found nowhere else in religious thought.

The Trinity is essential to Christianity because it reflects the relational nature of God. God is not a solitary being but a being of eternal love and fellowship. The Father loves the Son, the Son loves the Father, and the Holy Spirit is the bond of their love. When humans are invited into a relationship with God, they are invited into this divine love.

Christianity's View of Humanity and the World

Christianity teaches that humans were created in the image of God (Genesis 1:27), meaning that they possess dignity, free will, and moral responsibility. However, humanity is also fallen—separated from God by sin. This concept of sin is another crucial part of Christian belief.

Unlike some religious traditions that see sin as ignorance (as in Buddhism) or as merely the breaking of religious laws (as in Islam), Christianity sees sin as something deeper—a fundamental rupture in the relationship between humanity and God. Sin is not just about bad actions; it is a condition that affects the human heart, leading to selfishness, pride, and ultimately, death.

The solution to this problem, according to Christianity, is not self-effort but redemption through Jesus Christ. The crucifixion and resurrection of Jesus are the central events in Christian history because they provide the means by which humanity can be restored to God.

Christianity's Differences from Other Religions

It is often said that all religions are fundamentally the same and only superficially different. But this is simply not true. While there are similarities between Christianity and other faiths—such as the emphasis on morality, prayer, and the search for the divine—Christianity stands apart in three key ways:

The Incarnation – No other religion claims that God became human. In Hinduism, divine avatars appear, but they are not the same as the Christian understanding of God permanently taking on human nature in Jesus.

Grace vs. Works – Almost all religions teach that human beings must strive to reach God. Christianity uniquely teaches that God reaches out to humanity first, offering salvation as a free gift.

The Resurrection – Christianity is built on a historical claim: that Jesus rose from the dead. Unlike myths or legends, Christianity asserts this as a real event, witnessed by many, and foundational to the faith (1 Corinthians 15:14).

What Does It Mean to Be a Christian?

To be a Christian is not merely to agree with certain doctrines or attend church services. It is to enter into a living relationship with Jesus Christ, trusting in him as Lord and Savior. This involves:

Faith – Believing in Christ's death and resurrection as the basis for salvation.

Repentance – Turning away from sin and aligning one's life with God.

Baptism – The outward sign of entering the Christian community.

Discipleship – Following Christ daily, growing in love and obedience.

At its core, Christianity is not just a belief system, but a way of life—a journey of transformation. It is about knowing God personally, being changed by his love, and sharing that love with others.

This is the essence of Christianity: not rules, not rituals, not philosophy—but a life-changing encounter with Jesus Christ, the Son of God, who calls all people into a relationship with him.

The Bible: Old and New Testaments

The structure, content, and authority of the Bible, including key translations.

Among the sacred texts of the world, the Bible stands as one of the most influential, complex, and widely read books in history. It has shaped civilizations, inspired countless works of art, guided moral thought, and served as the foundational document of Christianity. But what exactly is the Bible? Where did it come from? How is it structured? And why do Christians regard it as authoritative?

To fully understand Christianity, one must begin with the Bible, for it is the source of Christian doctrine, history, and moral instruction. The Bible is not a single book but rather a collection of books, written by various authors over the course of many centuries. It is divided into two main parts:

The Old Testament – which records God's dealings with humanity, particularly through the nation of Israel, before the coming of Jesus Christ.

The New Testament – which documents the life, death, and

resurrection of Jesus, as well as the teachings of his earliest followers.

Together, these two sections form a narrative of divine revelation, showing how God has acted throughout history to bring about salvation for the world.

The Structure of the Bible

The Bible contains 66 books in the Protestant tradition, while Catholic and Orthodox versions include additional books known as the Deuterocanonical books or Apocrypha. The books of the Bible vary in genre, including history, law, poetry, prophecy, wisdom literature, and personal letters.

The Old Testament

The Old Testament, also known as the Hebrew Scriptures, is the larger of the two sections, containing 39 books (in the Protestant canon). It was written primarily in Hebrew, with some portions in Aramaic. The Old Testament can be divided into four main sections:

The Pentateuch (Torah or Law) – The first five books (Genesis, Exodus, Leviticus, Numbers, Deuteronomy) attributed to Moses. These books describe creation, the fall of humanity, the formation of Israel, and the laws given by God.

The Historical Books – Books such as Joshua, Judges, 1 & 2 Samuel, and 1 & 2 Kings recount the history of Israel, including its triumphs and failures.

The Wisdom and Poetry Books – Including Job, Psalms, Proverbs, Ecclesiastes, and Song of Solomon, these books focus on worship, wisdom, and human struggles.

The Prophets – Divided into Major Prophets (Isaiah, Jeremiah, Ezekiel, Daniel) and Minor Prophets (Hosea, Joel, Amos, etc.), these books contain messages from God through prophets warning, encouraging, and foretelling the coming of the Messiah.

The Old Testament lays the groundwork for the New Testament, introducing themes such as sin, sacrifice, covenant, prophecy, and the expectation of a Savior.

The New Testament

The New Testament, written in Greek, consists of 27 books that center around Jesus Christ and the early Christian Church. It is also divided into four main sections:

The Gospels – Matthew, Mark, Luke, and John provide four accounts of Jesus' life, teachings, miracles, crucifixion, and resurrection. Each Gospel offers a unique perspective on Jesus, with Matthew emphasizing Jesus as the Jewish Messiah, Mark highlighting his power and authority, Luke focusing on his compassion and inclusion of the marginalized, and John presenting a more theological portrait of Jesus as the Son of God.

The Acts of the Apostles – Written by Luke, Acts serves as a continuation of the Gospel of Luke and details the birth and expansion of the early Church, particularly the work of Peter and Paul.

The Epistles (Letters) – These 21 letters, written by apostles such as Paul, Peter, James, and John, provide instruction, encouragement, and theological insight to early Christian communities. Paul's letters, such as Romans, 1 & 2 Corinthians, and Galatians, articulate key doctrines like justification by faith, the role of grace, and Christian living.

The Book of Revelation – A highly symbolic and prophetic book, Revelation presents visions of the end times, the final victory of Christ, and the new heaven and new earth.

The New Testament fulfills the Old Testament by showing how Jesus is the promised Messiah and by establishing the new covenant between God and humanity.

The Authority of the Bible

Christians regard the Bible as authoritative, but different traditions understand this authority in slightly different ways. Evangelical Protestants emphasize Sola Scriptura ("Scripture alone"), meaning that the Bible is the final and highest authority in matters of faith. Catholics and Orthodox Christians, while highly revering Scripture, also recognize the authority of Sacred Tradition and the teaching authority of the Church.

Why is the Bible considered authoritative? Several reasons are given:

Divine Inspiration – Christians believe that the Bible is "God-breathed" (2 Timothy 3:16). This does not mean that God dictated it word-for-word, but that the human authors wrote under the guidance of the Holy Spirit.

Historical Reliability – The Bible has been remarkably well-preserved through thousands of manuscripts, some dating to within a century of the original writings.

Fulfilled Prophecy – The Old Testament contains hundreds of prophecies that Christians believe were fulfilled in Jesus Christ.

Transformative Power – Throughout history, countless individuals have testified that reading the Bible changed their lives.

Key Translations of the Bible

Because the Bible was originally written in Hebrew, Aramaic, and Greek, it has been translated into nearly every language in the world. Some of the most significant translations include:

The Septuagint (LXX) – A Greek translation of the Old Testament, widely used in the early Church.

The Vulgate – A Latin translation completed by St. Jerome in the 4th century, used by the Catholic Church for over a thousand years.

The King James Version (KJV) – One of the most famous English translations, published in 1611, known for its majestic and poetic style.

The New International Version (NIV) – A modern English translation that balances accuracy with readability.

The English Standard Version (ESV) – A word-for-word translation that seeks to preserve the original meaning while maintaining clarity.

Each translation has its strengths, and different Christian traditions prefer different versions based on factors like readability, theological emphasis, and textual accuracy.

Conclusion

The Bible is the foundation of Christian belief, serving as a sacred text, a historical record, and a theological guide. It is divinely inspired, historically reliable, and deeply transformative. The Old Testament tells the story of humanity's creation, fall, and the unfolding plan of salvation through Israel. The New Testament reveals the fulfillment of that plan in Jesus Christ, offering hope and redemption to all who believe.

Understanding the Bible—its structure, content, and authority—is essential for anyone seeking to comprehend Christianity. Whether read devotionally, studied academically, or analyzed historically, the Bible remains the most influential and enduring book in human history.

God in Christianity: The Trinity

The doctrine of the Father, Son, and Holy Spirit.

Among the most profound and mysterious doctrines of Christianity is the belief in the Trinity—the idea that the one true God exists in three persons: Father, Son, and Holy Spirit. This concept is both central to Christian theology and one of the most difficult to comprehend fully. While the word Trinity itself does not appear in the Bible, the doctrine emerges from the scriptural witness and has been a foundational belief of Christianity since its earliest days.

The Trinity distinguishes Christianity from all other monotheistic religions. Judaism and Islam, while affirming one God, reject the idea of a triune deity as incompatible with strict monotheism. Hinduism and other polytheistic traditions, on the other hand, allow for multiple deities but lack the concept of one divine essence shared among three persons. Thus, the Christian view of God is unique in religious history, presenting a paradox that has captivated theologians for centuries.

To understand the Trinity, we must explore what Christians believe about God's nature, how this belief developed, and how it impacts Christian life and worship.

The Biblical Foundation of the Trinity

Although the Bible never explicitly lays out a doctrine of the Trinity in a systematic way, both the Old and New Testaments contain elements that point to the triune nature of God.

The Old Testament Hints at the Trinity

The Old Testament firmly establishes the oneness of God. One of the most famous declarations in Judaism is the Shema, found in Deuteronomy 6:4:

"Hear, O Israel: The Lord our God, the Lord is one."

This verse became the foundation of Jewish monotheism and remains central to Christian belief. However, scattered throughout the Old Testament are hints of plurality within God's nature:

Genesis 1:26 - "Then God said, Let us make man in our image, after our likeness." The plural pronouns us and our suggest a complexity within God's being.

Isaiah 9:6 - The prophet Isaiah, foretelling the coming of the Messiah, calls him "Mighty God, Everlasting Father," suggesting divine attributes for a future figure.

Isaiah 48:16 - "And now the Lord God has sent me, and his Spirit." This verse speaks of three entities: the Lord, the speaker (often understood as the Messiah), and the Spirit.

These passages do not explicitly teach the Trinity, but they lay the groundwork for the fuller revelation that comes in the New Testament.

The New Testament and the Full Revelation of the Trinity

The clearest teaching of the Trinity emerges in the New Testament, particularly in the life, ministry, and teachings of Jesus Christ.

The Baptism of Jesus - One of the most vivid depictions of the Trinity occurs when Jesus is baptized (Matthew 3:16-17):

Jesus, the Son, is baptized in the Jordan River.

The Holy Spirit descends like a dove.

The Father speaks from heaven: "This is my beloved Son, in whom I am well pleased."

Here, all three persons of the Trinity are present and distinct.

The Great Commission - Before ascending to heaven, Jesus commands his disciples:

"Go therefore and make disciples of all nations, baptizing them in the name of the Father and of the Son and of the Holy Spirit." (Matthew 28:19)

The singular "name" (not "names") suggests that the Father, Son, and Holy Spirit share one divine identity.

The Apostolic Benediction – The Apostle Paul frequently speaks of all three persons together, as in 2 Corinthians 13:14:

"The grace of the Lord Jesus Christ, and the love of God, and the communion of the Holy Spirit be with you all."

These passages, among many others, make it clear that Jesus and the Holy Spirit are not mere creations of God, but fully divine persons who share in the identity of the one God.

Understanding the Trinity: Three in One

The doctrine of the Trinity affirms that:

There is only one God – Christianity is monotheistic (Deuteronomy 6:4).

God exists as three distinct persons – The Father, the Son (Jesus), and the Holy Spirit.

Each person is fully God – The Father is God, the Son is God, and the Holy Spirit is God.

The three persons are not separate gods but one being.

To illustrate, early Christian theologians used analogies, though none perfectly explain the mystery:

The Sun – The Father is like the sun, the source of light; the Son is the rays of light that reach the earth; the Holy Spirit is the warmth we feel.

Water – Water can exist as ice, liquid, and steam, yet it remains H_2O.

Human Relationships – A person can be a father, a son, and a brother at the same time, though this analogy risks suggesting modalism (the false belief that God simply changes forms).

Heresies and Misunderstandings of the Trinity

Throughout history, various heresies (false teachings) have arisen concerning the Trinity. The early Church had to defend the true doctrine against these errors:

Modalism – The belief that God is one person who appears in three different modes (Father, Son, and Spirit) at different times, rather than existing as three persons simultaneously. This view denies the personal relationships within the Trinity.

Arianism – Taught by Arius in the 4th century, Arianism claimed that Jesus was not fully divine but rather the first created being. This led to the Council of Nicaea (325 AD) and the formulation of the Nicene Creed, which affirmed that Christ is "of the same substance" (homoousios) as the Father.

Tritheism – The mistaken belief that the Father, Son, and Holy Spirit are three separate gods. This distorts the oneness of God.

The Trinity in Christian Life and Worship

The doctrine of the Trinity is not merely an abstract theological concept; it has profound practical implications for Christian life and worship.

Prayer – Christians pray to the Father, through the Son, by the power of the Holy Spirit.

Salvation – The Father sends the Son, the Son redeems, and the Holy Spirit applies salvation to the believer's life.

Worship – True Christian worship is Trinitarian, glorifying Father, Son, and Spirit. Hymns, liturgies, and prayers often reflect this reality.

Conclusion

The Trinity is one of the deepest mysteries of the Christian faith, yet it is also one of its most essential doctrines. It distinguishes Christianity from all other religious systems, affirms the complexity and relational nature of God, and serves as the foundation for Christian belief and practice.

From the Old Testament hints to the New Testament revelation, from theological disputes to deep devotional life, the Trinity stands at the heart of Christian faith. It is a doctrine not fully comprehensible by human reason but one that invites us into the mystery of divine love—the eternal relationship of Father, Son, and Holy Spirit.

 ## Jesus Christ: His Life and Mission

The historical and theological significance of Jesus, his teachings, and his impact.

The figure of Jesus Christ stands at the very heart of Christianity. His name is the foundation upon which the faith is built, his life the model for Christian living, and his mission the cornerstone of the Christian understanding of salvation. Across centuries, billions have turned to Jesus as the Son of God, the Savior, and the embodiment of divine truth and love.

Yet, Jesus is more than a theological concept or a religious leader; he is also an undeniable historical figure. Unlike the mythical gods of antiquity, Jesus of Nazareth walked the earth, spoke to multitudes, challenged the powerful, and left an indelible mark on human civilization. His teachings have shaped the moral fabric of the West, his example has inspired movements of compassion and justice, and his claim to be the Son of God has been the subject of both profound devotion and fierce debate.

To understand Jesus Christ fully, we must examine both the historical and theological significance of his life, from his birth to his death and resurrection, as well as the mission that defined his time on earth.

The Historical Jesus: Birth and Early Life

The story of Jesus begins in the most humble of settings. According to the Gospels of Matthew and Luke, Jesus was born in Bethlehem, a small Judean town, during the reign of King Herod the Great. His mother, Mary, was a young Jewish woman who conceived him by the

Holy Spirit, and his earthly father, Joseph, was a carpenter from Nazareth, a small village in Galilee.

The Gospels tell of Jesus' birth as the fulfillment of Old Testament prophecy, particularly Isaiah 7:14, which foretells that a virgin will conceive and give birth to a son called Emmanuel, meaning "God with us." From the very beginning, Jesus' life was marked by divine purpose.

But his arrival was not welcomed by all. Herod, fearing the prophecy of a newborn "king of the Jews," ordered the massacre of male infants in Bethlehem in an attempt to eliminate him. Joseph, warned in a dream, fled with Mary and Jesus to Egypt, where they remained until Herod's death.

After returning to Israel, Jesus grew up in Nazareth, working in Joseph's trade as a carpenter. Unlike other great religious leaders, Jesus did not receive formal theological training nor was he part of the Jewish priesthood. His early years remain largely a mystery, apart from a brief account of his visit to the Temple in Jerusalem at the age of twelve (Luke 2:41-50), where he astonished the teachers with his wisdom.

Jesus' Public Ministry

At the age of about thirty, Jesus began his public ministry, following his baptism by John the Baptist in the Jordan River. This event marked the beginning of his mission. As he emerged from the water, the Holy Spirit descended upon him "like a dove," and a voice from heaven declared, "This is my beloved Son, in whom I am well pleased" (Matthew 3:16-17).

From that moment, Jesus set out to proclaim the Kingdom of God, heal the sick, cast out demons, and call people to repentance. His teachings were radical, challenging the religious and social norms of his time. He gathered a group of twelve disciples, ordinary men—fishermen, tax collectors, and zealots—who would become his closest followers and the foundation of the early Church.

The Teachings of Jesus

At the core of Jesus' message was the concept of the Kingdom of God—not a political kingdom, but a spiritual reality in which God reigns supreme. His teachings emphasized:

Love and Compassion – Jesus taught that love was the greatest commandment: love for God and love for neighbor (Matthew 22:37-40). He extended this even to enemies, a revolutionary idea at the time (Matthew 5:44).

Forgiveness and Grace – Unlike the rigid legalism of the religious authorities, Jesus proclaimed that sinners could be forgiven, illustrating this through parables such as the Prodigal Son (Luke 15:11-32).

Humility and Servanthood – He overturned worldly expectations by declaring that the greatest among people were those who served others (Mark 10:45).

Faith Over Ritual – Jesus often clashed with the Pharisees, condemning their hypocrisy and emphasizing inner righteousness over external religious observances (Matthew 23).

The Promise of Eternal Life – He proclaimed himself to be "the way, the truth, and the life" (John 14:6), promising eternal life to those who believed in him.

Jesus spoke in parables, simple yet profound stories that conveyed deep spiritual truths. These parables—such as the Good Samaritan, the Mustard Seed, and the Lost Sheep—illustrated the nature of God, human responsibility, and the path to salvation.

Miracles and Signs

Jesus' ministry was not just one of words but of action. He performed numerous miracles that demonstrated his divine power:

Healing the blind, the lame, and the lepers.

Raising the dead, including Lazarus.

Feeding thousands with only a few loaves and fish.

Walking on water and calming storms.

Casting out demons, showing his authority over spiritual forces.

These miracles were not simply displays of power; they were signs pointing to his divine identity and the breaking in of God's kingdom on earth.

The Conflict and the Road to the Cross

As Jesus' influence grew, so did the opposition against him. The Jewish religious leaders—the Pharisees, Sadducees, and scribes—saw him as a threat. He exposed their hypocrisy, disregarded their strict traditions, and even claimed authority over the Temple itself.

The final turning point came when Jesus entered Jerusalem for the last time, riding on a donkey while crowds hailed him as the Messiah. This event, known as the Triumphal Entry, enraged the religious authorities.

Shortly after, Jesus shared the Last Supper with his disciples, instituting what would become the Christian practice of Communion (Luke 22:19-20). That same night, he was betrayed by Judas Iscariot, arrested, and brought before the Jewish council. Accused of blasphemy for claiming to be the Son of God, he was handed over to Pontius Pilate, the Roman governor.

Despite Pilate finding no guilt in him, Jesus was sentenced to death by crucifixion, the most brutal form of Roman execution. He was scourged, mocked, and forced to carry his own cross to Golgotha, where he was crucified between two criminals.

Theological Significance of Jesus' Death

Christians believe that Jesus' crucifixion was not just a tragic miscarriage of justice but the fulfillment of God's plan of salvation. According to Christian doctrine:

Jesus took upon himself the sins of the world, offering himself as the ultimate sacrifice (Isaiah 53:5-6).

His death fulfilled Old Testament prophecies, such as the suffering servant of Isaiah 53.

Through his sacrifice, he reconciled humanity with God, bridging the gap caused by sin.

As Jesus breathed his last, he cried out, "It is finished" (John 19:30), signifying that his work of redemption was complete.

The Resurrection: The Triumph Over Death

But the story does not end in death. Three days later, Jesus rose from the dead. His resurrection is the foundation of Christian faith, proving his divinity and victory over sin and death. He appeared to his disciples, teaching them and commissioning them to spread the Gospel.

After forty days, he ascended into heaven, promising to return. His followers, emboldened by this reality, went out and transformed the world.

Conclusion

The life and mission of Jesus Christ are the foundation of Christianity. He was not just a teacher or a prophet, but the Son of God, the Savior of the world. His message of love, forgiveness, and eternal life continues to shape lives and societies.

Whether viewed as a historical figure or as the risen Lord, Jesus Christ remains the most influential person in human history.

The Crucifixion and Resurrection

The central event of Christianity and its theological implications.

Christianity stands or falls on the reality of the crucifixion and resurrection of Jesus Christ. This is not merely an event in history but the defining moment of the Christian faith, shaping its theology, its message, and its mission. The crucifixion is the culmination of human sin and divine love, while the resurrection is the vindication of Jesus' identity and the ultimate victory over death itself.

The Apostle Paul, one of the most influential figures in early Christianity, emphasized this truth when he wrote:

"And if Christ has not been raised, then our preaching is in vain, and your faith is in vain" (1 Corinthians 15:14).

Without the crucifixion, there is no atonement for sin. Without the resurrection, there is no hope of eternal life. Together, these events form the centerpiece of Christian belief, not just as historical occurrences but as spiritual realities that affect every human being.

To fully grasp their significance, we must examine the historical background, the events themselves, and the deep theological implications they hold for salvation, justice, grace, and the destiny of humanity.

The Road to the Cross: The Crucifixion of Jesus

The Historical and Political Context

By the time of Jesus' crucifixion, Judea was under Roman occupation, and tensions were high between the Jewish people and their rulers. The Romans allowed limited religious freedom, but any sign of rebellion was met with swift and brutal punishment. The Jewish leaders, particularly the Pharisees and Sadducees, sought to preserve their authority and maintain peace with the Romans.

Jesus, with his radical teachings, growing popularity, and claims of divine authority, was a direct challenge to both the religious and political establishment. He was viewed as a threat by the Jewish leaders and as a potential political insurgent by the Romans.

During his final week in Jerusalem, Jesus entered the city to the shouts of crowds who hailed him as the Messianic King—a fulfillment of ancient Jewish prophecies. This event, known as the Triumphal Entry, alarmed the religious elite, who saw his influence growing dangerously strong.

The Betrayal and Arrest

One of Jesus' own disciples, Judas Iscariot, agreed to betray him to the Jewish authorities for thirty pieces of silver—a sum that eerily fulfilled an Old Testament prophecy (Zechariah 11:12-13). After the Last Supper, where Jesus instituted the practice of the Eucharist (Communion), he went to the Garden of Gethsemane to pray.

It was here, in the agony of anticipation, that Jesus wrestled with the reality of what was to come. Luke's Gospel tells us that he was so distressed that "his sweat became like great drops of blood falling to the ground" (Luke 22:44). This highlights the profound psychological and spiritual weight of the cross before him.

Moments later, Judas arrived with a band of soldiers, identifying Jesus with a kiss. He was arrested and taken before the Sanhedrin, the Jewish ruling council.

The Trials and Condemnation

Jesus was subjected to multiple trials, first before the Jewish leaders and then before the Roman governor, Pontius Pilate.

The Jewish authorities accused him of blasphemy—claiming to be the Son of God.

Before Pilate, the charge shifted to treason—declaring himself "King of the Jews," which was a direct challenge to Caesar's authority.

Pilate found no fault in Jesus, but under pressure from the crowds—whipped into a frenzy by the religious leaders—he reluctantly condemned him to death. To symbolize his reluctance, Pilate washed his hands before the people, declaring, "I am innocent of this man's blood" (Matthew 27:24).

The Suffering of the Cross

Crucifixion was the most brutal form of Roman execution, reserved for the worst criminals. It was designed not just to kill but to inflict maximum suffering and humiliation. Before being crucified, Jesus was:

Severely flogged—a punishment so extreme that many did not survive it.

Mocked and beaten by Roman soldiers, who placed a crown of thorns on his head and clothed him in a purple robe, sarcastically calling him "King of the Jews."

Forced to carry his own cross to Golgotha, the site of execution.

At Golgotha, he was nailed to the cross, his wrists and feet pierced with iron spikes. For six hours, he hung there in excruciating pain, gasping for breath as he endured the jeers of onlookers.

At the moment of his death, Jesus cried out:

"It is finished" (John 19:30).

This was not a cry of defeat, but of completion—his mission was fulfilled.

The Gospel accounts tell us that at the moment of his death:

The veil in the Temple was torn in two, symbolizing the end of separation between God and humanity.

A great earthquake shook the land.

A Roman centurion, witnessing the event, declared, "Truly, this was the Son of God!" (Matthew 27:54).

The Resurrection: The Triumph Over Death

The story does not end with the crucifixion. Three days later, Jesus rose from the dead—an event that changed history forever.

The Empty Tomb

Early on Sunday morning, Mary Magdalene and other women went to Jesus' tomb to anoint his body. But when they arrived, they found the stone rolled away and the tomb empty.

An angel proclaimed to them:

"Why do you seek the living among the dead? He is not here, but has risen!" (Luke 24:5-6).

This news spread quickly, and soon Jesus began to appear to his disciples, proving that he was truly alive.

Eyewitness Accounts

The Apostle Paul, writing within two decades of the resurrection, lists those who encountered the risen Christ:

Mary Magdalene (John 20:14-16).

The disciples on the road to Emmaus (Luke 24:13-35).

The Apostle Thomas, who doubted until he saw Jesus' wounds (John 20:24-29).

Over 500 people at one time (1 Corinthians 15:6).

For forty days, Jesus appeared, taught, and prepared his followers before ascending into heaven.

The Theological Significance of the Crucifixion and Resurrection

The crucifixion and resurrection are not just historical events; they carry profound theological implications:

Atonement for Sin – Jesus' death was the sacrifice that paid the price for human sin, fulfilling the Old Testament system of sacrifices.

Victory Over Death – The resurrection proves that death is not the end and that eternal life is possible through Christ.

The Foundation of Christian Hope – If Christ rose, his followers will also rise (1 Corinthians 15:20-22).

Divine Justice and Love – The cross demonstrates God's justice (sin is punished) and God's love (he took the punishment himself).

Conclusion

The crucifixion and resurrection of Jesus Christ define Christianity. They are historically attested, theologically profound, and personally transformative for all who believe.

This is why Christians do not just worship a dead martyr—they follow a living Savior.

Salvation and Grace

The Christian understanding of sin, redemption, and grace.

Christianity is, at its core, a religion of salvation. More than a philosophy, more than a moral code, it is a faith built upon the idea that human beings are fallen, in need of rescue, and that God, in His boundless love, has provided that rescue through Jesus Christ. This salvation is not earned through effort, nor is it deserved; rather, it is given freely by grace—a concept that stands in contrast to nearly every other religious system in history.

To understand the Christian doctrine of salvation and grace, one must first understand the problem it seeks to solve: sin. Without sin, there is no need for redemption, and without redemption, grace loses its meaning. From the earliest pages of the Bible to the teachings of Christ and the letters of the apostles, the themes of sin, salvation, and grace form the backbone of the Christian narrative.

The Problem of Sin: Humanity's Separation from God

The Bible begins with a grand vision of creation. God, in His infinite goodness, brings forth the heavens and the earth, fashioning humanity in His own image (Genesis 1:26-27). Man and woman were created not merely as biological beings but as spiritual creatures, meant to live in communion with their Creator.

Yet, this harmony was shattered by sin. The story of Adam and Eve in Genesis 3 tells of the first rebellion against God—the first assertion of human pride against divine authority. By eating the fruit of the Tree of the Knowledge of Good and Evil, they introduced disobedience, suffering, and death into the world. This act was not merely a mistake; it was a deliberate rejection of God's will.

From that moment onward, sin became the condition of the human race. It is not simply about wrong actions but about a fundamental brokenness, a separation from the holiness of God. The Apostle Paul puts it starkly:

"For all have sinned and fall short of the glory of God" (Romans 3:23).

Sin affects every part of human life—our desires, our relationships, our institutions. It creates alienation between humanity and God, between people themselves, and even within the human heart. In the Old Testament, this separation was addressed through the law and sacrifices, but these were temporary measures, unable to fully restore what had been lost. The solution, Christians believe, would come not through human effort, but through divine intervention.

The Work of Christ: Redemption Through the Cross

Into this world of sin and brokenness came Jesus Christ, whom Christians believe to be the Son of God and the Savior of the world. His mission was not merely to teach moral principles but to bring salvation—to restore humanity's relationship with God.

Jesus' entire ministry was an act of redemption. He healed the sick, forgave sins, and proclaimed the arrival of the Kingdom of God—a reality in which the power of sin was being undone. Yet, the ultimate act of salvation occurred through his death on the cross and his resurrection from the dead.

The Meaning of the Cross

The crucifixion of Jesus is not just a tragic event or a political execution—it is the pivotal moment in salvation history. The Bible teaches that Jesus' death was a sacrifice for sin, fulfilling the role of the Old Testament sacrifices that temporarily covered human transgressions. In Christ, however, the sacrifice was final and complete.

Paul explains this in his letter to the Romans:

"But God demonstrates His own love toward us, in that while we were still sinners, Christ died for us" (Romans 5:8).

In other words, salvation is not something we achieve; it is something that God accomplishes on our behalf. The cross is where divine justice and mercy meet:

Justice, because sin is not ignored; it is paid for.

Mercy, because humanity is spared the punishment it deserves.

Jesus' resurrection, then, is the proof of victory. If death was the consequence of sin, then Christ's resurrection declares that sin has been defeated. This is why Christians believe that salvation is not only about forgiveness but also about new life. Those who trust in Christ are not only pardoned but are made new creations (2 Corinthians 5:17).

Grace: The Undeserved Gift of Salvation

At the heart of Christian salvation is a radical and counterintuitive idea: grace.

Most religious traditions operate on the principle of earning salvation through good deeds, obedience, or enlightenment. Christianity, however, proclaims that salvation is a gift—one that cannot be earned but only received.

Paul states it clearly:

"For by grace you have been saved through faith, and that not of yourselves; it is the gift of God, not of works, lest anyone should boast" (Ephesians 2:8-9).

This means that:

Salvation is not based on human merit. No amount of good works can make a person righteous before God.

Salvation is offered freely by God's love. It is His initiative, not ours.

Salvation is received by faith, trusting in Christ alone.

This doctrine was one of the central issues of the Protestant Reformation. Martin Luther, John Calvin, and others emphasized Sola Gratia—"by grace alone"—arguing against the idea that human efforts could contribute to salvation.

Yet, grace does not mean license to sin. Paul anticipated this objection when he wrote:

"Shall we continue in sin that grace may abound? Certainly not!" (Romans 6:1-2).

Rather, grace transforms. A person who has received God's grace is called to live in response to it, not out of fear of punishment, but out of love and gratitude.

The Role of Faith and Works in Salvation

One of the longest-standing debates in Christian theology is the relationship between faith and works. If salvation is by grace alone, where do good works fit in?

The New Testament offers a balanced perspective:

Faith alone justifies – A person is made right with God through faith in Christ, not through works (Romans 3:28).

Good works are the fruit of salvation – True faith results in a changed life, marked by love, holiness, and service (James 2:26).

James famously wrote:

"Faith without works is dead" (James 2:26).

This is not a contradiction to Paul's teaching on grace. Rather, James emphasizes that true faith naturally produces good works. Works do not save, but they demonstrate the reality of salvation.

The Universality of Salvation: Who Can Be Saved?

A crucial element of Christian teaching is that salvation is available to all. Unlike some religious traditions that restrict salvation to a certain ethnic or moral elite, Christianity declares that anyone who believes in Christ can be saved.

"Whoever calls on the name of the Lord shall be saved" (Romans 10:13).

This universality makes Christianity radically inclusive:

It is not limited by nationality or race (Galatians 3:28).

It is not reserved for the righteous—Jesus himself welcomed sinners, tax collectors, and outcasts.

It is not hindered by past sins—the Apostle Paul, a former persecutor of Christians, became one of its greatest evangelists.

Conclusion: The Call to Respond

Salvation is the greatest gift of God to humanity. It is the answer to the problem of sin, the fulfillment of God's love, and the foundation of Christian hope. But like any gift, it must be received.

The New Testament repeatedly calls people to respond:

"Repent and believe in the gospel" (Mark 1:15).

Christianity does not merely offer a set of rules; it offers a new life—one founded on grace, secured by Christ, and available to all who trust in Him.

This is the essence of the Christian message: that sinners can be redeemed, that grace is freely given, and that through Jesus Christ, humanity is reconciled to God.

Christian Eschatology: The End Times

Heaven, hell, judgment, and the second coming of Christ.

Christianity has always been a forward-looking faith, one that speaks not only to the present but also to the ultimate destiny of humanity and the world. Eschatology—the study of the "last things" or the "end times"—is one of the most compelling and controversial aspects of Christian theology. It addresses profound questions: What happens after death? Is there an ultimate judgment? What will become of the world? Will justice ever be fully realized?

For Christians, these questions find their answers in the second coming of Christ, the resurrection of the dead, the final judgment, and the eternal destiny of souls in either heaven or hell. These beliefs, drawn from both the Old and New Testaments, have shaped Christian thought, influenced cultures, and even sparked movements throughout history.

The Biblical Foundations of Christian Eschatology

Eschatological themes run throughout the Bible, but they become most explicit in the prophetic books of the Old Testament and the apocalyptic literature of the New Testament.

The Old Testament contains early glimpses of eschatology, particularly in the prophets (Isaiah, Daniel, Ezekiel) who spoke of a future where God would judge the wicked, restore Israel, and establish His kingdom.

The New Testament, particularly the teachings of Jesus, the writings of Paul, and the Book of Revelation, expands and clarifies these ideas, foretelling Christ's return, the final judgment, and the renewal of creation.

At the heart of Christian eschatology is the promise of Christ's return, an event that will mark the fulfillment of God's plan for history and the ushering in of a new, perfected existence.

The Second Coming of Christ

One of the most central beliefs in Christian eschatology is that Jesus Christ will return to the world in glory. This belief is rooted in Jesus' own words:

"Then will appear the sign of the Son of Man in heaven. And then all the peoples of the earth will mourn when they see the Son of Man coming on the clouds of heaven, with power and great glory." (Matthew 24:30)

Christians believe that at this second coming (parousia), Christ will defeat evil, judge the living and the dead, and establish God's eternal kingdom.

However, there is significant debate among Christian traditions regarding the exact nature and timing of Christ's return.

Some traditions emphasize imminence, believing Christ could return at any moment.

Others see his return as following a series of prophetic events, such as the rise of the Antichrist, a period of tribulation, and a final climactic battle between good and evil.

Despite these differences, the certainty of Christ's return is a fundamental doctrine shared by all Christian denominations.

The Resurrection of the Dead

Closely tied to Christ's return is the belief in the resurrection of the dead. Christianity teaches that death is not the end, and that all people will one day be raised from the dead to face judgment.

Paul speaks of this in 1 Corinthians 15, describing how the perishable human body will be transformed into an imperishable one:

"For the trumpet will sound, the dead will be raised imperishable, and we will be changed." (1 Corinthians 15:52)

This resurrection is not just spiritual but also bodily—a radical assertion that emphasizes the goodness of God's creation and His intent to restore it. Christians believe that those who belong to Christ will be resurrected to eternal life, while others will face final judgment.

The Final Judgment

The final judgment is another cornerstone of Christian eschatology. This is the moment when God will judge every person according to their deeds. The righteous will be rewarded, and the wicked will face eternal separation from God.

Jesus himself describes this judgment vividly:

"Then he will say to those on his left, 'Depart from me, you who are cursed, into the eternal fire prepared for the devil and his angels.'" (Matthew 25:41)

This judgment is depicted as both just and merciful—just, because evil and injustice will be held accountable, and merciful, because God offers salvation to those who accept His grace.

Heaven and Hell: The Eternal Destinies

Following the final judgment, all souls will enter their eternal state, either in heaven or hell.

Heaven: The Fulfillment of God's Kingdom

Heaven is described as a place of unimaginable joy and unity with God. It is often depicted in Revelation 21 as the New Jerusalem, where:

There will be no more suffering, pain, or death.

God will dwell among His people.

Humanity will live in perfect love, peace, and joy.

Heaven is not merely a location—it is the fulfillment of humanity's deepest longing to be with God and to be transformed into His likeness.

Hell: The Reality of Separation from God

In contrast, hell is often depicted as a place of eternal separation from God. Some Christian traditions view it as literal torment, while others interpret it as spiritual alienation from God.

Jesus spoke about hell in graphic terms—as a place of darkness, fire, and regret (Matthew 8:12, Mark 9:43). Yet, the fundamental idea is that hell is not an arbitrary punishment—it is the natural consequence of rejecting God's love and grace.

Some Christian traditions also hold to alternative views, such as:

Annihilationism: The belief that the wicked will ultimately cease to exist rather than suffer eternally.

Universalism: The belief that all souls will ultimately be reconciled to God.

The New Heaven and New Earth: The Restoration of Creation

Beyond personal judgment and destiny, Christian eschatology also speaks of a renewed creation. The final vision in the Book of Revelation is not of souls escaping to heaven, but of heaven and earth becoming one.

"Then I saw a new heaven and a new earth, for the first heaven and the first earth had passed away." (Revelation 21:1)

This vision suggests that God's plan is not to destroy the world but to redeem it, perfect it, and dwell with His people forever. It is not an escape from the material world but its transformation.

Different Interpretations of the End Times

Throughout history, Christians have debated the exact timeline and events leading to the end. Some of the major eschatological frameworks include:

Premillennialism: The belief that Christ will return before a literal thousand-year reign.

Postmillennialism: The belief that the world will gradually improve through Christian influence before Christ's return.

Amillennialism: The belief that the millennium is symbolic, and that Christ's kingdom is already present in a spiritual sense.

These differing views have led to diverse interpretations of prophecy, but they all agree on the fundamental Christian hope: God will ultimately triumph over evil, and His people will dwell with Him forever.

Conclusion: A Call to Hope and Readiness

Christian eschatology is not meant to instill fear but to offer hope. It reminds believers that history is moving toward a divine purpose, that justice will be done, and that suffering is not the final word.

At the same time, the uncertainty of the timeline serves as a call to readiness. As Jesus said:

"Therefore keep watch, because you do not know on what day your Lord will come." (Matthew 24:42)

For Christians, the message is clear: Live faithfully, love deeply, and stand firm in hope—for the end is not the end, but the beginning of eternity.

✝ The Early Church: From Apostles to Councils

The growth of Christianity after Jesus' death, including persecution and the formation of doctrine.

Christianity was born in the crucible of the ancient world, a small movement centered around a crucified Jewish teacher in the Roman province of Judea. Within a few centuries, it grew into a powerful force that reshaped the Roman Empire and beyond. But the road from Jesus' resurrection to the establishment of Christianity as a dominant world religion was anything but smooth. It was marked by intense persecution, theological disputes, missionary expansion, and the gradual formation of Christian doctrine.

This section explores the critical developments in the early Church, from the apostolic era to the great councils that defined Christian belief for centuries to come.

The Apostolic Age: The Church Begins (33–100 AD)

The Christian movement began with the resurrection of Jesus and the empowerment of his followers at Pentecost (Acts 2), when the Holy Spirit descended upon the apostles. These first Christians were Jewish believers, initially seeing themselves as a reform movement within Judaism rather than a new religion.

However, several key developments quickly set Christianity apart:

The preaching of the apostles spread Jesus' message throughout the Roman Empire.

The inclusion of Gentiles (non-Jews) into the faith, particularly through the missionary work of Paul.

The shift from Jewish law to a new covenant, based on faith in Christ rather than adherence to Mosaic law.

The Missionary Journeys and the Growth of the Church

Among the apostles, one figure stands out: Paul of Tarsus. A former persecutor of Christians, Paul had a dramatic conversion experience (Acts 9) and became the most influential missionary in the early Church.

He traveled across Asia Minor, Greece, and Rome, establishing churches and writing letters (epistles) that would later become part of the New Testament.

His teaching emphasized salvation through faith in Christ rather than adherence to Jewish law, a major theological shift.

His work helped Christianity spread beyond Jewish communities and become a universal faith.

By the end of the first century, Christian communities had been established in major cities across the Roman Empire, including Rome, Antioch, Corinth, and Alexandria.

Persecution Under Rome: The Blood of the Martyrs (64–313 AD)

Christianity was not welcomed by Roman authorities. Unlike Judaism, which was legally tolerated, Christianity was viewed as a dangerous sect.

Several factors led to its persecution:

Christians refused to worship the Roman gods or the Emperor, which was seen as treason.

Rumors spread that Christians were atheists and cannibals (due to misunderstandings about the Eucharist).

Christianity's rapid growth alarmed Roman leaders, who saw it as a potential threat to stability.

The first major persecution occurred under Emperor Nero (64 AD), who blamed Christians for the Great Fire of Rome. Other emperors, including Domitian, Decius, and Diocletian, also launched brutal crackdowns.

Despite this, persecution only strengthened the Church. The

courage of martyrs such as Ignatius of Antioch, Polycarp, and Perpetua inspired many to convert. The famous saying, "The blood of the martyrs is the seed of the Church" (Tertullian), reflects how persecution fueled the movement rather than destroyed it.

The Formation of the New Testament (90-200 AD)

As the Church grew, so did the need for authoritative teachings. The first Christians relied on:

The Hebrew Scriptures (Old Testament).

The oral teachings of Jesus and the apostles.

Letters (epistles) from early Christian leaders.

By the late 2nd century, certain texts were widely recognized as authoritative Scripture, including the four Gospels (Matthew, Mark, Luke, John) and Paul's letters.

However, disagreements over which books should be included led to the gradual formation of the New Testament canon, finalized in the 4th century.

The Age of Apologists and Theologians (100-313 AD)

As Christianity spread, it encountered intellectual and theological challenges from both pagan philosophers and heretical movements. Early Christian thinkers—known as Apologists—defended the faith through reason and philosophy.

Key Apologists and Their Contributions

Justin Martyr (100-165 AD): Argued that Christianity was the fulfillment of Greek philosophy.

Irenaeus of Lyons (130-202 AD): Defended Christian doctrine against Gnostic heresies.

Tertullian (160-225 AD): Coined the term "Trinity" to describe God as Father, Son, and Holy Spirit.

These thinkers helped shape Christian theology and defend it against false teachings.

The Rise of Heresies and the Need for Orthodoxy

As the Church expanded, heresies (false teachings) arose, requiring clear doctrinal responses.

Gnosticism: Claimed secret knowledge (gnosis) was needed for salvation, rejecting the physical world as evil.

Marcionism: Rejected the Old Testament and taught that the God of Israel was not the true God.

Arianism (later): Denied the full divinity of Jesus.

To combat heresy, the Church developed creeds (formal statements of belief) and ecclesiastical authority through bishops.

The Turning Point: Constantine and the Edict of Milan (313 AD)

A seismic shift occurred in 313 AD, when Emperor Constantine the Great issued the Edict of Milan, legalizing Christianity and ending centuries of persecution.

Constantine, after a vision of a cross before battle, converted to Christianity.

He granted Christians freedom of worship and returned confiscated church property.

He called the First Council of Nicaea (325 AD) to settle disputes about Jesus' divine nature.

Christianity transitioned from a persecuted minority to an imperial religion, setting the stage for its dominance in Europe.

The First Ecumenical Councils (325–451 AD): Defining Christian Doctrine

As Christianity became official, doctrinal unity became a major concern. The early Church faced internal divisions over theology, leading to ecumenical councils—large gatherings of bishops to settle debates.

The Council of Nicaea (325 AD): The Divinity of Christ

Called by Constantine to settle the Arian controversy.

Arius claimed Jesus was created by God and not co-eternal.

The council affirmed Jesus as "of the same essence" (homoousios) as the Father.

Produced the Nicene Creed, which remains foundational to Christian belief.

The Council of Chalcedon (451 AD): The Nature of Christ

Resolved debates about whether Jesus had one or two natures.

Affirmed that Christ is fully God and fully man, a doctrine known as the Hypostatic Union.

These councils defined orthodoxy, creating a unified doctrine for the global Church.

Conclusion: The End of the Early Church Era

By the end of the 5th century, Christianity had:

Grown from a small Jewish sect to the dominant faith of the Roman Empire.

Survived intense persecution and theological disputes.

Established its core doctrines through councils and creeds.

Developed into a structured, hierarchical Church led by bishops.

The early Church laid the foundation for all of Christianity. From its missionary zeal to its doctrinal battles, from persecution to imperial favor, it was a time of dramatic change and defining moments.

The Church was now prepared to enter a new era—the medieval age—where it would shape the world in ways no one could have foreseen.

The Formation of Christian Doctrine

The key councils (Nicaea, Chalcedon, etc.) and the development of creeds.

Christianity, from its inception, was a faith in motion—a movement born in the streets of Jerusalem and quickly carried into the heart of the Greco-Roman world. But with expansion came challenges. The earliest followers of Jesus had to grapple with fundamental questions: Who was Jesus? How was he related to God? What did salvation mean? What defined true Christian belief?

These were not merely abstract theological puzzles. They were questions that shaped the very core of Christian identity. The early Church was not a monolithic institution but a diverse and sometimes fractious collection of believers, stretching across the Mediterranean, encountering different cultures, philosophies, and interpretations of Jesus' message. As Christianity spread, disagreements arose, heresies emerged, and conflicting teachings threatened to divide the young faith.

To address these issues, the early Church turned to councils—gatherings of bishops and theologians tasked with defining doctrine and resolving disputes. Over time, these councils formulated the great creeds of Christianity—statements of belief that continue to define Christian orthodoxy today.

The Need for Doctrinal Clarity

The first Christians were Jews who saw Jesus as the fulfillment of God's promises. But as Gentiles entered the faith, new questions arose. Who exactly was Jesus? Was he divine? Was he created? Was he equal to God?

Some believers, following Arianism, argued that Jesus was a

created being, distinct from God. Others insisted that Jesus was fully divine, co-eternal with the Father. These were not minor disagreements—they struck at the heart of Christianity. If Jesus was merely a creation of God, then the doctrine of salvation was in question.

At the same time, other groups, such as the Gnostics, claimed that Jesus had only appeared to be human, denying his full humanity. Others denied the Trinity, while some insisted that Christ had only one nature rather than both divine and human. These theological disputes threatened to tear the Church apart.

In response, Christian leaders convened councils—large gatherings of bishops who would debate, pray, and ultimately issue authoritative decisions on doctrine. The result was a series of ecumenical councils, which forged the foundational beliefs of Christianity.

The Council of Nicaea (325 AD): The Battle Over Christ's Divinity

The first and perhaps most significant council was the Council of Nicaea, convened in 325 AD by Emperor Constantine. Constantine, having legalized Christianity through the Edict of Milan (313 AD), sought unity in the empire—and Christian theological disputes were causing division.

The main issue at Nicaea was Arianism, the teaching of a priest named Arius, who argued that Jesus was not of the same essence as God but was rather the first and greatest of God's creations. Arius's famous phrase was:

"There was a time when the Son was not."

This meant that Jesus, though divine in some sense, was not fully God. His opponent, Athanasius of Alexandria, vehemently disagreed, arguing that Jesus was fully divine, co-equal, and co-eternal with the Father.

The council ruled in favor of Athanasius, affirming that Christ was homoousios ("of the same essence") as the Father. The result was the Nicene Creed, a declaration of faith that affirmed the full divinity of Jesus and condemned Arianism.

The Nicene Creed (excerpts):

"We believe in one God, the Father Almighty, Maker of heaven and earth... And in one Lord Jesus Christ, the only-begotten Son of God, begotten of the Father before all worlds, God of God, Light of Light, very God of very God; begotten, not made, being of one substance with the Father..."

This creed remains central to Christianity today, recited in churches across the world. However, the Arian controversy did not disappear, and further councils were needed to clarify Christ's nature.

The Council of Constantinople (381 AD): The Trinity Defined

Though Nicaea had established Christ's divinity, the Holy Spirit's role remained unclear. Some groups, known as Pneumatomachians ("Spirit-fighters"), argued that the Holy Spirit was not fully divine.

The Council of Constantinople reaffirmed Nicaea's teachings and expanded on them, declaring that the Holy Spirit was also fully God, forming the doctrine of the Trinity—one God in three persons: Father, Son, and Holy Spirit.

The Nicene Creed was expanded to reflect this:

"...And in the Holy Spirit, the Lord and giver of life, who proceeds from the Father, who with the Father and the Son together is worshiped and glorified..."

With this, the doctrine of the Trinity—the cornerstone of Christian theology—was firmly established.

The Council of Ephesus (431 AD): Mary, Theotokos

The next major controversy revolved around Mary and how she

should be understood in relation to Christ. The bishop Nestorius argued that Mary should not be called "Theotokos" (God-bearer, Mother of God), because she only gave birth to Jesus' human nature, not his divine nature.

The Council of Ephesus (431 AD) condemned Nestorianism, affirming that Christ was one person, fully divine and fully human, and that Mary could indeed be called "Mother of God."

This was crucial because it emphasized that Jesus was not two separate beings (one human, one divine), but one unified person.

The Council of Chalcedon (451 AD): The Two Natures of Christ

The next great debate centered on how Jesus' divine and human natures coexisted. Some, like the Monophysites, argued that Christ had only one nature (divine), absorbing his humanity. Others insisted on two separate persons in Christ.

The Council of Chalcedon (451 AD) settled the issue, declaring:

Jesus Christ is one person with two natures—fully divine and fully human, without confusion, change, division, or separation.

This doctrine, called the Hypostatic Union, remains a defining belief of Christianity.

The Legacy of the Councils and the Development of Christian Doctrine

These early councils were foundational in shaping Christian theology. They established:

The full divinity of Christ (Nicaea).

The Trinity—Father, Son, and Holy Spirit (Constantinople).

The unity of Christ's person (Ephesus).

The doctrine of Christ's two natures (Chalcedon).

The result was a strong, unified theological framework that still defines Christianity today.

However, the councils also led to schisms. Those who rejected Chalcedon's decision, like the Coptic and Syriac churches, split from the main Church. This foreshadowed later divisions, such as the Great Schism (1054 AD) and the Protestant Reformation (16th century).

Yet, despite these divisions, the core doctrines established by the early councils remain foundational to all branches of Christianity—Catholic, Orthodox, and Protestant alike.

Conclusion: The Defining Moment of Christian Orthodoxy

The formation of Christian doctrine was not a smooth or automatic process. It was forged in the fires of controversy, persecution, and theological struggle. But through it, Christianity emerged with a clear identity—one that defined its understanding of God, Christ, and salvation.

The councils and creeds established the essential beliefs of the faith, providing a foundation that has endured for nearly two millennia. Without them, Christianity might have splintered into countless sects with contradictory beliefs.

Instead, it became a global faith, rooted in the Nicene tradition, a testament to the enduring power of its doctrinal heritage.

The Great Schism: East and West

The division of Christianity into Roman Catholicism and Eastern Orthodoxy.

Few events in the history of Christianity have had as profound and long-lasting an impact as the Great Schism of 1054, the moment when the Christian Church, which had long been one united body, split into the Roman Catholic Church in the West and the Eastern Orthodox Church in the East. This division was not the result of a single event but rather the culmination of centuries of political, theological, and cultural differences.

The Great Schism was not merely a bureaucratic disagreement between religious leaders. It was a rift that had been widening for centuries, fueled by rivalries between Rome and Constantinople, disputes over theological doctrines, and conflicts between the Western Latin-speaking world and the Eastern Greek-speaking world. By the time of the official split, the Christian world had already been functioning as two separate entities, but the events of 1054 marked the definitive rupture, one that has persisted for nearly a millennium.

The Roots of the Schism: Political and Cultural Divides

The seeds of division between the Eastern and Western Christian worlds were planted as early as the 4th century when the Roman Emperor Constantine the Great relocated the capital of the empire from Rome to Byzantium, later renamed Constantinople (modern-day Istanbul), in 330 AD.

This move signaled a shift in power away from the old city of Rome. Over time, the Eastern Roman Empire (Byzantium) and the Western Roman Empire developed distinct political identities, languages, and cultures. The West remained under the influence of Latin-speaking Rome, while the East flourished as a Greek-speaking civilization with its own traditions and customs.

By the 5th century, the Western Roman Empire collapsed under the weight of barbarian invasions, while the Eastern Byzantine Empire endured for another thousand years. The Bishop of Rome (the Pope) in the West increasingly asserted authority over all of Christendom, while in the East, the Patriarch of Constantinople remained influential but did not claim universal supremacy.

This political shift contributed to tensions between the Church in Rome and the Church in Constantinople, as both centers vied for influence. While both were part of the broader Christian world, they increasingly saw themselves as separate entities.

Theological and Doctrinal Disputes

While political and cultural differences created an atmosphere of tension, it was theological disagreements that cemented the divide. Several doctrinal issues fueled the schism:

1. The Filioque Controversy: The Dispute Over the Holy Spirit

One of the most contentious doctrinal disputes was over a single Latin word: "Filioque", meaning "and the Son."

Originally, the Nicene Creed—established in 325 AD and confirmed at the Council of Constantinople in 381 AD—stated that the Holy Spirit proceeds from the Father. However, in the 6th century, the Western Church unilaterally added the phrase "and the Son" (Filioque) so that the creed read:

"...who proceeds from the Father and the Son."

The Eastern Church strongly objected to this addition, arguing that:

It violated the authority of the early ecumenical councils, which had declared the original creed to be unchangeable.

It altered the doctrine of the Trinity, making the Holy Spirit appear subordinate to both the Father and the Son.

For the Eastern Orthodox Church, this unauthorized change was a serious theological breach. They maintained that the Holy Spirit proceeds only from the Father, as originally stated in the creed.

The Western Church, however, insisted that the Filioque clause was necessary to clarify the relationship between the three persons of the Trinity. By the time of the Schism, the disagreement over the Filioque had become a defining symbol of the East-West divide.

2. Papal Supremacy vs. Conciliarism

Another major issue was the role and authority of the Pope.

The Bishop of Rome (the Pope) claimed to be the supreme leader of the entire Christian Church, asserting his authority based on Apostolic Succession from Saint Peter.

The Patriarch of Constantinople and other Eastern bishops, however, rejected this claim, believing that all bishops were equal in authority, with no single leader ruling over the entire Church.

The Eastern Church favored a conciliar model of leadership, where important theological decisions were made by ecumenical councils, rather than by a single bishop. The Western Church, under the Pope, moved toward a centralized system in which the Pope was seen as Christ's representative on Earth.

This conflict over papal authority was a fundamental point of rupture. The Pope saw himself as the unquestioned head of Christianity, while the Eastern leaders refused to submit to his authority.

3. Liturgical and Practical Differences

Even in the daily life of Christians, differences between East and West became increasingly apparent:

Language: The West conducted liturgy in Latin, while the East used Greek.

Clerical Marriage: In the West, priests were required to remain celibate, while in the East, married men could become priests (but not bishops).

Leavened vs. Unleavened Bread: The Eastern Church used leavened bread for the Eucharist, symbolizing the risen Christ, while the Western Church used unleavened bread, similar to Jewish Passover tradition.

These differences, though seemingly minor, reflected deeper cultural and theological divisions between the two branches of Christianity.

The Schism of 1054: A Moment of Formal Division

The final break came in 1054 AD, in a dramatic confrontation between the Pope and the Patriarch of Constantinople.

In that year, Pope Leo IX sent Cardinal Humbert to Constantinople to assert papal authority over the Eastern Church.

In response, Patriarch Michael Cerularius rejected the Pope's authority and closed Latin-speaking churches in Constantinople.

In a final act of defiance, Cardinal Humbert excommunicated Patriarch Cerularius in Hagia Sophia, the grand cathedral of Constantinople.

In turn, Patriarch Cerularius excommunicated the Pope.

This mutual excommunication marked the formal beginning of the Great Schism. From that point forward, the Roman Catholic Church and the Eastern Orthodox Church became separate entities.

Aftermath and Lasting Consequences

The Schism was not immediately felt by ordinary Christians, but over time, the divide between Eastern Orthodoxy and Roman Catholicism hardened.

The Crusades (especially the Fourth Crusade of 1204), in which Western Christian armies sacked Constantinople, deepened resentment between East and West.

Efforts at reconciliation (such as the Council of Florence in 1439) failed to bridge the theological and political gap.

The fall of Constantinople to the Ottoman Empire in 1453 further isolated the Eastern Church.

Today, the Great Schism remains one of the most enduring divisions in Christianity. Though relations between the two churches have improved—especially after the mutual lifting of excommunications in 1965—the Catholic and Orthodox Churches remain distinct branches of Christianity, each with its own traditions, leadership, and theological emphases.

Conclusion: A House Divided

The Great Schism of 1054 was not an isolated event—it was the culmination of centuries of political rivalries, cultural differences, and theological disagreements. At its core, it was a battle over authority and identity. Was the Church to be led by one supreme bishop (the Pope) or by a council of equals? Was the Holy Spirit proceeding from the Father alone or from the Father and the Son?

Despite the divisions, Catholicism and Orthodoxy share a common foundation—both affirm the Trinity, the divinity of Christ, and the authority of Scripture. But the Schism serves as a reminder of the fragility of unity and the profound consequences of unresolved disputes.

The Protestant Reformation

Martin Luther, John Calvin, and the rise of Protestantism.

The Protestant Reformation was one of the most transformative events in Christian history, a revolution that shattered the unity of Western Christendom and reshaped religious, political, and cultural landscapes. It was not merely a theological dispute—it was a movement that altered the course of European history, challenging the authority of the Roman Catholic Church, redefining the nature of faith, and inspiring new denominations that would spread across the globe.

At the heart of the Reformation stood Martin Luther, a German monk whose fiery critique of the Catholic Church ignited a movement that could not be contained. Following him, John Calvin, with his systematic theology and emphasis on divine sovereignty, provided the intellectual foundation for the Reformation's continued expansion. But these were not the only figures involved—throughout Europe, new voices arose, each contributing to the birth of Protestant Christianity.

The Corruption of the Late Medieval Church

By the early 16th century, the Catholic Church was the most powerful institution in Europe. The Pope wielded immense influence over both spiritual and secular affairs, and the clergy was deeply enmeshed in political intrigues. However, many Christians, including priests and scholars, had grown increasingly disillusioned with widespread corruption within the Church.

The selling of indulgences was one of the most controversial practices at the time. Indulgences were documents issued by the Church that promised to reduce the punishment for sins, and they were often sold for money. Pope Leo X, in particular, aggressively promoted indulgences to fund the construction of St. Peter's Basilica in Rome, an act that outraged many believers.

In addition to indulgences, other signs of corruption were rampant: Simony: The buying and selling of church offices.

Nepotism: Church positions being given to family members rather than qualified individuals.

Clerical Immorality: Many priests lived extravagant lives, violating vows of celibacy and engaging in questionable financial dealings.

These issues, combined with growing humanist influences from the Renaissance, led scholars and theologians to rethink the role of the Church and its authority.

Martin Luther and the Birth of the Reformation
The 95 Theses: A Challenge to Rome

The Reformation officially began on October 31, 1517, when Martin Luther, a German monk and professor of theology, nailed his 95 Theses to the church door in Wittenberg, Germany.

These 95 Theses were a direct challenge to the practice of indulgences and, more broadly, to the entire system of Church authority. Luther argued that:

Salvation comes through faith alone (sola fide)—not through indulgences or good works dictated by the Church.

The Bible, not the Pope, is the ultimate authority (sola scriptura).

All believers have direct access to God and do not require the mediation of priests.

At first, Luther sought reform within the Catholic Church, but when Pope Leo X excommunicated him in 1521, Luther refused to recant his teachings. Instead, he defied Rome and set the wheels of revolution in motion.

The Translation of the Bible and the Spread of Protestantism

One of Luther's most significant contributions was his translation of the Bible into German, allowing ordinary people to read the Word of

God in their own language for the first time.

This effort was part of a broader movement to make Christianity more accessible. With the advent of the printing press, Luther's ideas spread rapidly across Europe, inspiring reformers in other countries to take up the cause.

John Calvin and the Rise of Reformed Christianity

While Luther initiated the Reformation, John Calvin gave it intellectual depth and structure.

Born in France, Calvin was a brilliant scholar who fled to Switzerland to escape persecution. His most famous work, Institutes of the Christian Religion (1536), laid out a comprehensive Protestant theology, shaping what would become Reformed Christianity.

Key Teachings of Calvinism

Predestination – Calvin taught that God had already determined who would be saved and who would be damned. This doctrine, known as "double predestination", became a defining feature of Calvinist theology.

Sovereignty of God – Calvin emphasized that God's will was absolute, and human free will played little role in salvation.

The Priesthood of All Believers – Like Luther, Calvin rejected the hierarchical priesthood of Catholicism, arguing that all Christians had equal access to God.

A Strict Moral Code – Calvin established Geneva as a theocratic state, enforcing a rigorous moral order that banned gambling, dancing, and excessive luxury.

Calvin's ideas spread across Europe, influencing Scotland (through John Knox and Presbyterianism), the Netherlands, and parts of France (Huguenots).

The Fragmentation of Western Christianity

As the Reformation spread, different leaders emerged, each

interpreting Scripture in their own way. This led to the creation of multiple Protestant movements:

Lutheranism (Germany & Scandinavia) – Followers of Martin Luther's teachings, emphasizing justification by faith alone.

Calvinism (Switzerland, Scotland, Netherlands) – Focused on God's sovereignty and predestination.

Anglicanism (England) – A hybrid of Catholic and Protestant traditions, created when King Henry VIII broke away from Rome in 1534.

Anabaptists (Radical Reformers) – Advocated for adult baptism, separation of church and state, and pacifism.

The Catholic Counter-Reformation

The Catholic Church did not remain passive in the face of Protestantism. It responded with the Counter-Reformation, a movement that sought to:

Reaffirm Catholic doctrines at the Council of Trent (1545-1563).

Reform corruption within the clergy.

Combat Protestant ideas through institutions like the Jesuit Order.

The Counter-Reformation stopped the spread of Protestantism in some areas but could not reverse the division of Western Christianity.

The Lasting Impact of the Reformation

The Protestant Reformation was not just a religious movement—it transformed Europe's political and cultural landscape.

Political Consequences – The Reformation weakened the power of the Catholic Church, leading to religious wars, such as the Thirty Years' War (1618-1648).

Rise of Religious Pluralism – Europe was no longer united under one Church, leading to the eventual acceptance of religious diversity.

The Growth of Literacy – The translation of the Bible into vernacular languages led to increased literacy rates.

Foundations for Modern Democracy – Protestant emphasis on individual conscience and direct access to God laid the groundwork for democratic ideals.

Today, Protestantism remains one of the dominant branches of Christianity, with hundreds of millions of followers worldwide.

Conclusion: A Faith Reformed, A World Transformed

The Protestant Reformation was a revolution, breaking the monopoly of the Catholic Church and reshaping Christianity forever. Luther and Calvin did not just protest abuses in the Church—they redefined the very nature of faith. Their teachings set the stage for the modern religious landscape, where personal belief and scriptural authority remain central to Christian life.

Though initially a movement of division, the Reformation ultimately led to greater religious diversity, inspiring movements that would shape history for centuries to come.

Christianity in the Modern World

The impact of Christianity in the 20th and 21st centuries.

Few institutions in human history have demonstrated the endurance and adaptability of Christianity. In a world that has undergone radical transformations—two world wars, the rise and fall of empires, technological revolutions, and shifts in cultural and moral paradigms—Christianity has remained a powerful force, shaping societies and individuals alike. The 20th and 21st centuries have seen both the decline of Christianity in some regions and its explosive growth in others. It has been a time of intense challenges, but also of profound influence, as Christianity continues to engage with politics, science, secularism, and global crises.

This section explores the modern role of Christianity, its transformations, struggles, and ongoing relevance in today's world.

The Decline of Christianity in the West

One of the most defining trends of the modern era has been the decline of Christianity in traditionally Christian regions, particularly in Western Europe and North America. In the past, these societies were shaped by Christian values, and church attendance was a central part of life. However, the 20th century saw a sharp decline in religious observance, which has accelerated in the 21st century.

Factors Behind the Decline
The Rise of Secularism and Scientific Rationalism

The Enlightenment and Scientific Revolution paved the way for secular thought, which accelerated in the modern era.

Figures like Nietzsche, Darwin, and Freud challenged religious dogma, and many began to see Christianity as outdated or incompatible with science.

The Impact of the World Wars

The horrors of World War I and II shook people's faith. Many questioned the existence of a just and loving God in the face of mass death and destruction.

The Holocaust, in particular, forced deep theological reflection about the role of the Church and its historical relationship with anti-Semitism.

The Sexual Revolution and Changing Moral Values

The 1960s brought sweeping social change, including new attitudes toward sexuality, marriage, and gender roles.

Christian teachings on family, marriage, and sexual ethics were increasingly seen as restrictive or out of touch with modern values.

The Scandals Within the Church

Sexual abuse scandals involving priests, particularly in the Catholic Church, deeply damaged public trust in Christianity.

Corruption, financial scandals, and instances of authoritarianism within churches have led many to distance themselves from institutional religion.

The Rise of Individualism and Consumer Culture

In modern societies, faith is increasingly seen as a personal, private matter, rather than a communal or national identity.

Consumer culture, driven by capitalism, promotes materialism over spiritual reflection, making religion seem irrelevant to daily life.

These factors have led to the sharpest decline in church attendance in history. Countries like the United Kingdom, France, Germany, and Sweden have seen church attendance drop below 10%, and atheism or agnosticism is now a mainstream identity.

However, while Christianity shrinks in the West, it is growing rapidly in other parts of the world.

The Explosive Growth of Christianity in the Global South

While Western nations have secularized, the Global South—particularly Africa, Asia, and Latin America—has seen a massive explosion in Christian conversions. The statistics are striking:

In Africa, the Christian population has grown from 10 million in 1900 to over 600 million today.

In Latin America, once dominated by Catholicism, Pentecostal and evangelical movements have surged, often outpacing traditional denominations.

In China, despite government crackdowns, there are an estimated 100 million Christians, making it one of the largest Christian populations in the world.

Reasons for Christianity's Growth in the Global South
Missionary Efforts and Indigenous Movements

Protestant and Catholic missionaries have spread Christianity widely, but increasingly, local movements have taken over.

Pentecostal and Charismatic Christianity, emphasizing healing, personal experiences with God, and revivalism, resonates deeply with non-Western cultures.

Christianity as a Force of Social Change

In many developing countries, churches provide education, healthcare, and social services, filling gaps left by governments.

Christian communities often lead human rights efforts, advocating against corruption, human trafficking, and political oppression.

Christianity's Ability to Adapt

Unlike the West, where Christianity is often tied to historical institutions, in the Global South, Christianity has adapted to local cultures, incorporating indigenous traditions and languages into worship.

This trend suggests that while Christianity is fading in some regions, it is more alive than ever in others.

Christianity and Politics in the Modern World

Christianity's relationship with politics remains one of the most controversial and defining aspects of the modern era.

The United States: The Christian Right vs. Progressive Christianity

In the U.S., Christianity is deeply intertwined with politics. The rise of the Christian Right, particularly since the 1980s, has led many evangelical Christians to become involved in issues like:

Opposition to abortion and same-sex marriage

Support for religious liberty and conservative family values

Political alignment with right-wing politics

However, at the same time, progressive Christianity has emerged, focusing on:

Social justice, racial reconciliation, and economic inequality

Interfaith dialogue and inclusivity

Environmental stewardship and climate activism

This divide within Christianity has shaped U.S. elections and continues to be a battleground for theological and political debates.

Christianity and Authoritarian Regimes

In countries like Russia and China, Christianity faces significant political challenges.

In Russia, the Orthodox Church is closely aligned with Vladimir Putin's government, acting as a nationalist and conservative force.

In China, the government actively suppresses Christianity, fearing its influence as a counterweight to state power.

In both cases, Christianity is either co-opted by the state or seen as a threat to political control.

The Future of Christianity in the 21st Century

What does the future hold for Christianity? While secularization in the West seems irreversible, and Christianity's center of gravity has shifted to the Global South, some trends suggest that Christianity is evolving in unexpected ways.

The Rise of Digital Christianity

The internet has allowed Christian communities to thrive online, from YouTube sermons to virtual churches.

Social media has become a major tool for evangelism, especially among younger generations.

New Theological Movements

Interfaith dialogue is increasing, with Christians engaging in deeper conversations with Muslims, Hindus, and Buddhists.

Ecumenical movements (cooperation between different Christian denominations) are growing, attempting to unify the fragmented Church.

The Challenge of Postmodernism

The Western world's move toward postmodern thought, which denies absolute truths, has forced Christians to rethink how to communicate their faith in a skeptical age.

Christianity's Role in Humanitarian Work

Christian organizations remain among the largest providers of aid, disaster relief, and education worldwide.

The call to serve the poor and vulnerable remains a core Christian mission, ensuring its ongoing influence.

Conclusion: Christianity's Continuing Influence

Christianity in the modern world is paradoxical—in decline in some places, yet thriving in others. It has lost power in the West but gained new vitality in Africa, Asia, and Latin America. It has been shaken by scandals but continues to inspire millions in acts of faith, charity, and social transformation.

The coming decades will determine how Christianity navigates modernity, but one thing remains certain: Christianity, far from being a relic of the past, is still one of the most influential forces shaping the present and future of humanity.

✝ The Nature of Humanity and Sin

The doctrine of original sin and human nature.

To understand Christianity, one must begin with its vision of human nature—a vision that is both deeply tragic and profoundly hopeful. Christianity teaches that humanity is created in the image of God (Imago Dei), imbued with dignity, reason, and the capacity for love. Yet, alongside this divine imprint, there is also a darkness within—the corruption of sin. Christianity does not view humanity as simply good or evil, but as a paradoxical mixture of both: noble yet fallen, capable of love yet prone to destruction.

At the heart of this doctrine lies the concept of original sin, a theological cornerstone that has shaped Christian views on morality, salvation, and human purpose. What does it mean to be sinful? Are we doomed by an ancient curse, or is sin a choice we make every day? Christianity has wrestled with these questions for millennia, and the answers have had profound consequences for theology, culture, and individual faith.

This section explores the Christian understanding of human nature, the doctrine of original sin, and its implications for salvation, morality, and the human condition.

Human Nature: The Image of God and the Fall

Christianity begins with an exalted view of humanity: we are made in the image of God (Genesis 1:27). This concept, known as Imago Dei, is foundational to Christian anthropology. It means that humans:

Possess reason and free will, unlike animals, allowing them to engage in moral decision-making.

Are created for relationship, both with God and with one another.

Have intrinsic dignity, meaning that every human life is sacred, regardless of social status, wealth, or achievements.

But this divine image, Christianity teaches, has been marred by sin. The story of the Fall in Genesis 3 is central to understanding how Christianity explains the brokenness of the world. Adam and Eve, the first humans, lived in perfect harmony with God. However, through disobedience—eating from the forbidden tree—they introduced sin into the world, bringing spiritual and physical death.

The consequences of this act were catastrophic:

Separation from God – Humanity lost its original closeness with the Creator.

Moral Corruption – The tendency to sin became embedded in human nature.

Death and Suffering – Pain, toil, and mortality entered the human experience.

This doctrine—that all human beings inherit a sinful nature from Adam and Eve—is known as original sin.

The Doctrine of Original Sin

The doctrine of original sin is one of the most controversial and widely discussed aspects of Christian theology. It was formally articulated by St. Augustine of Hippo (354–430 AD), one of Christianity's greatest thinkers. Augustine argued that:

Adam's sin was not just personal, but transmitted to all humanity.

Human beings are born with a sinful nature, not just a tendency to sin but an innate corruption.

Only divine grace—not human effort—can restore humanity to its original goodness.

This idea was later developed by theologians such as Thomas Aquinas, Martin Luther, and John Calvin, each of whom contributed different perspectives on how sin affects free will and salvation.

Different Views on Original Sin

Over time, Christian traditions have debated the extent and impact of original sin:

Catholic View: Baptism removes the guilt of original sin, but the tendency to sin (concupiscence) remains.

Protestant View: Many Protestant traditions, particularly Reformed theology (Calvinism), emphasize total depravity—the idea that every aspect of human nature is affected by sin.

Eastern Orthodox View: The Orthodox Church does not emphasize inherited guilt but rather ancestral sin, seeing it more as a separation from divine grace than as a corrupt nature.

Despite these differences, all Christian traditions affirm that sin is a fundamental human problem, requiring divine intervention.

Sin in the Christian Life

Beyond original sin, Christianity speaks of personal sin, the daily moral failings that affect human relationships and spiritual life. These sins can be:

Sins of Commission (actively doing wrong, e.g., lying, stealing, harming others).

Sins of Omission (failing to do good, e.g., neglecting the poor, failing to act justly).

Christianity also categorizes sin in different ways:

Venial vs. Mortal Sin (Catholic Tradition)

Venial sins are minor wrongdoings that weaken the soul but do not sever one's relationship with God.

Mortal sins are grave offenses (such as murder or adultery) that cut one off from grace unless repented.

Seven Deadly Sins (Medieval Christian Thought)

Medieval Christianity further explored sin through the concept of the Seven Deadly Sins, which became a moral framework:

Pride – Arrogance and self-exaltation.
Greed – Obsession with material wealth.
Lust – Disordered sexual desire.
Envy – Resentment of others' success.
Gluttony – Excessive indulgence.
Wrath – Uncontrolled anger.
Sloth – Spiritual laziness.

These sins were contrasted with the Seven Virtues—humility, generosity, chastity, kindness, temperance, patience, and diligence.

Sin and Redemption: The Need for Salvation

Christianity does not leave humanity condemned in sin. The central message of the gospel is that sin is conquered through Jesus Christ.

The Incarnation – God became human in Christ to restore the fallen world.

The Crucifixion – Christ's death is seen as a sacrifice for sin, taking on the punishment humans deserve.

The Resurrection – Christ's victory over death signifies a new creation, where sin will be fully overcome.

Justification and Sanctification

Christianity describes two key aspects of redemption:

Justification – The moment of being declared righteous by God (through faith and grace).

Sanctification – The ongoing process of overcoming sin and growing in holiness.

While different Christian traditions emphasize faith (Protestant) or faith plus works (Catholic/Orthodox), all agree that salvation requires God's grace.

The Struggle Against Sin: A Lifelong Battle
Even after salvation, Christians believe in an ongoing struggle against sin. The Apostle Paul famously described this inner conflict in Romans 7:15-20:

"For what I want to do I do not do, but what I hate I do."

Christianity teaches that grace enables believers to overcome sin, but it requires effort:

Prayer and Sacraments – Tools of grace that strengthen the soul.
Confession and Repentance – Continual turning away from sin.
Spiritual Warfare – Resisting temptation and the influence of evil.

Conclusion: The Christian Vision of Humanity
Christianity presents a complex but hopeful view of humanity. While sin has corrupted human nature, it has not erased the image of God within us. The Christian message is ultimately one of redemption, not despair—that through Christ, humans can be transformed, restored, and ultimately united with God.

The doctrine of original sin explains the brokenness of the world, but Christianity's promise is that sin does not have the final word. The last word belongs to grace, love, and divine redemption.

The Role of Faith and Works

The theological debate on salvation through faith versus works.

One of the most profound and enduring debates in Christian theology revolves around a central question: What does it mean to be saved? Is salvation a gift freely given, received through faith alone, or is it something that must be earned through good works and righteous living? This debate, often framed as faith versus works, has shaped Christian doctrine, divided churches, and influenced countless believers seeking to understand their spiritual standing before God.

To fully grasp the complexity of this issue, we must explore its biblical roots, its development through church history, and the various positions held by different Christian traditions.

The Biblical Foundation: Faith and Works in Scripture

The tension between faith and works is evident in the Bible itself, with different passages emphasizing different aspects of salvation. Two of the most frequently cited texts in this debate are:

Ephesians 2:8-9 (Faith Alone Emphasized)

"For it is by grace you have been saved, through faith—and this is not from yourselves, it is the gift of God—not by works, so that no one can boast."

James 2:24 (Works as Necessary)

"You see that a person is justified by works and not by faith alone."

These two verses appear, at first glance, to be in direct contradiction with one another. Paul, in Ephesians, strongly emphasizes that salvation is an act of divine grace, received through faith, and not something humans can achieve by their own merits. Yet James, in his epistle, insists that faith without works is dead—suggesting that belief alone is insufficient unless it is accompanied by actions.

This apparent tension has been interpreted in different ways throughout Christian history, leading to distinct theological positions on the relationship between faith, works, and salvation.

Early Christianity: A Unified Vision of Faith and Works

In the earliest days of the Christian church, faith and works were seen as inseparable. The apostolic teachings encouraged believers to have faith in Christ while also living virtuous and charitable lives.

The words of Jesus Himself point to a faith that is active rather than passive:

Matthew 7:21: "Not everyone who says to me, 'Lord, Lord,' will enter the kingdom of heaven, but only the one who does the will of my Father who is in heaven."

Matthew 25:34-40 (The Parable of the Sheep and the Goats) – Jesus explicitly ties acts of mercy to salvation, stating that caring for the poor, hungry, and imprisoned is the mark of true righteousness.

For the early church, the issue was not faith versus works but faith expressed through works. This balance is seen in the teachings of Church Fathers such as Augustine, who emphasized grace but also insisted that Christians must cooperate with it through righteous living.

The Protestant Reformation: The Rise of "Faith Alone" (Sola Fide)

The great turning point in the faith vs. works debate came during the Protestant Reformation of the 16th century. Martin Luther, one of the central figures of the Reformation, argued vehemently that salvation comes by faith alone (sola fide), apart from any human effort.

Luther's Protest Against "Works-Based Salvation"

Luther's primary concern was the Roman Catholic Church's

teaching that works—such as sacraments, penance, and indulgences—played a role in salvation. He saw this as a corruption of the biblical doctrine of grace. His key points were:

Salvation is by faith alone (sola fide).

Works do not contribute to justification but rather flow naturally from true faith.

The church had wrongly emphasized human effort, leading to abuses such as selling indulgences (where people could "buy" reduced punishment for sins).

Luther's famous Ninety-Five Theses (1517) challenged the Church's emphasis on works, and he used Paul's writings in Romans and Galatians to defend his stance.

John Calvin and Predestination

Another key Reformer, John Calvin, built on Luther's ideas but took them further with the doctrine of predestination. Calvin taught that:

Salvation is entirely a work of God (monergism).

Good works are evidence of salvation, but not a requirement for it.

The elect (those predestined for salvation) will naturally produce good works as a sign of their faith.

Thus, in Reformed theology, works are a byproduct of faith rather than a means to salvation.

The Catholic Response: Faith and Works Together

The Protestant challenge forced the Catholic Church to clarify its stance on faith and works. In the Council of Trent (1545-1563), the Church reaffirmed that:

Faith is essential, but it must be accompanied by works.

Justification begins with grace, but humans must cooperate with that grace.

Good works—such as acts of charity, sacraments, and obedience—play a role in maintaining salvation.

The Catholic position rejects both extreme legalism (works without faith) and extreme antinomianism (faith without works). Instead, it embraces what is often called synergism—the idea that God's grace and human effort work together in salvation.

Modern Perspectives: A Growing Middle Ground

While historical conflicts have shaped denominational divides, many modern Christians recognize the complexity of the issue. Today, there is a broader consensus that:

Faith is primary, but it must manifest in works.

Works are not a way to "earn" salvation, but they are the fruit of a genuine relationship with Christ.

Grace is necessary, but believers must respond to it through action.

Many Protestants now acknowledge James' argument that true faith will always lead to works. At the same time, many Catholics emphasize that works are only possible through God's grace, avoiding the idea of earning salvation by human effort alone.

Conclusion: A Faith That Works

Ultimately, the debate over faith and works is not merely academic—it has real implications for how Christians live their lives.

If salvation were by faith alone, with no requirement for works, then ethical behavior and moral living might seem secondary. If salvation were by works alone, then faith in Christ would be unnecessary, and salvation would be a matter of human achievement.

Christianity offers a profound alternative: faith that transforms lives and leads to action. As the Apostle Paul wrote:

"For in Christ Jesus neither circumcision nor uncircumcision has any value. The only thing that counts is faith expressing itself through love." (Galatians 5:6)

This, perhaps, is the best way to resolve the tension—not faith or works, but faith that works.

The Church: Its Role and Function

The nature of the Church, its sacraments, and its mission.

At the heart of Christianity stands the Church—not merely a building or an institution, but a living, breathing community of believers. For over two millennia, the Church has served as the body of Christ on earth, the place where faith is nurtured, sacraments are celebrated, and the mission of Jesus Christ continues. It has been a force of unity and division, a beacon of hope and sometimes a source of controversy. To understand Christianity, one must understand the Church: its nature, sacraments, and mission.

The Nature of the Church: More Than an Institution

The word "church" is derived from the Greek ekklesia, meaning "assembly" or "gathering". In the New Testament, it does not refer to a physical structure but rather to the people of God—those called out from the world to follow Christ. Jesus Himself spoke of the Church in Matthew 16:18, saying:

"And I tell you that you are Peter, and on this rock, I will build my church, and the gates of Hades will not overcome it."

This passage has been widely interpreted as Jesus instituting a community of faith that would endure through history. But what is this community's purpose?

The Church as the Body of Christ

The Apostle Paul provided one of the most compelling metaphors for the Church in 1 Corinthians 12:27:

"Now you are the body of Christ, and each one of you is a part of it."

In this vision, the Church is not an organization ruled by human hierarchy alone; rather, it is an extension of Christ's presence in the world. Every believer has a role to play—some as teachers, some as servants, some as leaders—but all working together for the greater mission of God.

The Church as the Bride of Christ

Another powerful image is that of the Church as the Bride of Christ (Ephesians 5:25-27). This portrays the relationship between Christ and His followers as a divine marriage, marked by love, commitment, and purity. The Church, like a bride, is being prepared for the return of Christ, growing in holiness and faithfulness.

The Sacraments of the Church: Signs of God's Grace

From its earliest days, the Church has administered sacraments—sacred rituals believed to convey God's grace. While different Christian traditions recognize varying numbers of sacraments, the two most universally accepted are:

1. Baptism: The Entrance into the Church

Baptism is the initiation rite of Christianity, symbolizing spiritual cleansing, rebirth, and membership in the faith.

Jesus Himself was baptized (Matthew 3:13-17), setting an example for His followers.

In the Great Commission (Matthew 28:19), Jesus commanded His disciples to baptize all nations in the name of the Father, Son, and Holy Spirit.

Different traditions practice baptism differently—some immerse, some sprinkle—but all see it as a mark of entry into the Christian life.

2. The Eucharist (Holy Communion): The Church's Central Act of Worship

The Eucharist, also called the Lord's Supper or Holy Communion, is a reenactment of Jesus' Last Supper. In it, Christians partake of bread and wine (or substitutes), symbolizing the body and blood of Christ.

Jesus instituted this sacrament in Luke 22:19-20, saying:

"Do this in remembrance of me."

Catholics believe in transubstantiation (the bread and wine become the actual body and blood of Christ).

Protestants interpret it more symbolically, as a reminder of Christ's sacrifice.

Despite theological differences, Communion remains the heart of Christian worship, uniting believers in remembrance, thanksgiving, and fellowship.

Other Sacraments

While Protestants typically recognize only Baptism and Communion, the Catholic and Orthodox Churches also include:

Confirmation (strengthening of faith)

Confession (Reconciliation) (forgiveness of sins)

Marriage (sacred union between man and woman)

Holy Orders (ordination of priests and deacons)

Anointing of the Sick (spiritual and sometimes physical healing)

These sacraments are seen as means through which God's grace flows, nurturing believers throughout their lives.

The Mission of the Church: Bringing Christ to the World

Beyond worship and sacraments, the Church has a global mission—to spread the message of Christ, serve humanity, and build God's kingdom on earth.

1. Evangelization: Preaching the Gospel

One of the Church's primary roles is evangelization—sharing the good news of Jesus Christ. This stems from Jesus' Great Commission (Matthew 28:19-20):

"Go therefore and make disciples of all nations, baptizing them in the name of the Father and of the Son and of the Holy Spirit, teaching them to observe all that I have commanded you."

Through missionary work, preaching, and personal witness, Christians have spread the gospel to every continent.

2. Charity and Social Justice: Serving the Poor and Needy

Christianity has long been a force for social change. The early Church was known for caring for widows, orphans, and the poor (Acts 6:1-7). This tradition continues today in:

Hospitals and schools founded by churches

Charities like the Salvation Army and Catholic Relief Services

Movements for justice, such as the abolition of slavery and civil rights

Jesus' words in Matthew 25:35-40 serve as the Church's guiding principle:

"For I was hungry and you gave me food, I was thirsty and you gave me drink, I was a stranger and you welcomed me."

3. Unity and Disunity: The Church as a Divided Body

Though called to be one body, the Church has seen many divisions—from the Great Schism (1054 AD) that split Eastern Orthodoxy and Roman Catholicism to the Protestant Reformation (1517 AD) that created numerous denominations.

Yet despite differences, most Christian groups still acknowledge:

The centrality of Jesus Christ

The authority of the Bible

A shared mission to spread God's love

In the modern world, efforts toward Christian unity (ecumenism) continue, seeking to heal divisions while respecting doctrinal differences.

Conclusion: The Church as a Living Reality

The Church is not just an institution—it is a living, spiritual reality that has shaped human history. It is a place of worship and teaching, sacraments and service, community and transformation.

At times, the Church has failed in its mission—succumbing to corruption, division, and hypocrisy. But at its best, it has been the presence of Christ on earth, lifting the poor, healing the broken, and calling humanity to a higher purpose.

As long as there are believers, the Church will continue—a beacon of faith, a vessel of grace, and a witness to the eternal love of God.

Christian Worship and Liturgy

Prayer, sacraments, and worship practices across denominations.

From the earliest days of Christianity, worship has been at the heart of the faith. It is in worship that believers express their devotion to God, find spiritual renewal, and commune with the divine. Across centuries and cultures, Christian worship has taken on many forms, yet at its core, it remains a response to the love and grace of God.

The rhythms of worship—whether expressed through quiet contemplation, solemn liturgy, or exuberant praise—have shaped the spiritual lives of millions. The sacraments, the prayers, and the rituals of Christianity are more than mere traditions; they are the expressions of faith that bind believers to God and to one another.

To understand Christian worship is to grasp the soul of the Church, the place where doctrine becomes experience, where theology takes on life, and where believers throughout history have come together in an intimate encounter with God.

The Foundations of Christian Worship

The first Christians did not gather in grand cathedrals or formal church buildings. Their worship took place in humble homes, often in secret due to persecution. They followed the example set by Jesus and the apostles, meeting together to pray, read scripture, break bread, and encourage one another. Acts 2:42 captures this beautifully:

"They devoted themselves to the apostles' teaching and to fellowship, to the breaking of bread and to prayer."

This early model of worship remains foundational:

Prayer as a means of connection with God.

The reading of Scripture as a way to learn and grow.

Communion (the Eucharist) as a shared remembrance of Christ.

Fellowship as a source of encouragement and accountability.

As Christianity spread, worship evolved—becoming more structured, incorporating formal prayers, and developing liturgical traditions that still shape Christian worship today.

Prayer: The Lifeblood of Worship

At the center of Christian worship is prayer—the intimate dialogue between the believer and God. Christianity has never been a religion of empty rituals or mere recitations; rather, it has emphasized a personal relationship with God.

Types of Christian Prayer

Prayer in Christian worship can take many forms, depending on the tradition and the occasion. Some of the most common include:

Liturgical Prayer – Set prayers, such as the Lord's Prayer, prayed in unison by congregations.

Personal Prayer – A spontaneous, heartfelt conversation with God.

Intercessory Prayer – Praying on behalf of others.

Contemplative Prayer – Silent, meditative communion with God, as seen in monastic traditions.

Charismatic Prayer – A Spirit-led, often extemporaneous prayer, frequently practiced in Pentecostal and Charismatic churches.

One of the most unifying elements of Christian worship is the Lord's Prayer, given by Jesus Himself in Matthew 6:9-13:

"Our Father in heaven, hallowed be your name, your kingdom come, your will be done, on earth as it is in heaven..."

Whether whispered in solitude or spoken in unison with

thousands, prayer remains the beating heart of Christian worship.

The Sacraments: Visible Signs of an Invisible Grace

The sacraments are sacred rites that Christians believe convey God's grace in a tangible way. They are the sacred moments in which the divine intersects with human life.

The Two Universally Recognized Sacraments

Though Christian traditions differ in their understanding of sacraments, two are universally recognized across denominations:

Baptism – The entrance into the Christian faith.

The Eucharist (Holy Communion) – The commemoration of Christ's death and resurrection.

Baptism: The Initiation into the Christian Life

Jesus Himself was baptized in the Jordan River (Matthew 3:13-17), and He commanded His followers to do likewise:

"Go and make disciples of all nations, baptizing them in the name of the Father and of the Son and of the Holy Spirit." (Matthew 28:19)

Different Christian traditions approach baptism in different ways:

Catholics, Orthodox, and many Protestants baptize infants, seeing baptism as a sign of God's covenant.

Baptists and other Evangelicals practice believer's baptism, where one is baptized after a personal confession of faith.

Some churches practice immersion, while others use sprinkling or pouring.

Despite these differences, baptism remains the entryway into the Christian community, a symbol of rebirth and new life.

The Eucharist: The Central Act of Worship

The Eucharist, also known as Holy Communion, the Lord's Supper, or the Mass, is the most sacred act of Christian worship. It is rooted in Jesus' Last Supper, where He took bread and wine and declared:

"This is my body, given for you; do this in remembrance of me." (Luke 22:19)

Christians interpret the Eucharist differently:

Catholics and Orthodox believers hold to the doctrine of transubstantiation, believing that the bread and wine become the actual body and blood of Christ.

Lutherans believe in consubstantiation, where Christ is spiritually present alongside the elements.

Protestants (such as Baptists and Evangelicals) see it as a symbolic memorial of Christ's sacrifice.

Regardless of interpretation, Communion remains a deeply sacred moment, reminding believers of Christ's love, sacrifice, and return.

Worship Practices Across Christian Denominations

Christian worship varies widely across traditions and denominations, reflecting different theological emphases, historical developments, and cultural influences.

1. Liturgical Worship (Catholic, Orthodox, and High-Church Protestantism)

In Catholic, Orthodox, and some Anglican or Lutheran churches, worship is highly structured and liturgical, marked by:

Formal prayers

Chanting and hymns

Incense, vestments, and processions

A central focus on the Eucharist

2. Evangelical and Charismatic Worship

Many Evangelical, Pentecostal, and Charismatic churches embrace a free-form, contemporary style of worship, characterized by:

Spontaneous prayers and sermons

Lively music, often with guitars and drums

Emotional expressions, such as raised hands or speaking in tongues

A strong emphasis on personal experience with the Holy Spirit

3. Monastic and Contemplative Worship

In monastic communities, such as those of the Benedictines, Franciscans, or Eastern Orthodox monks, worship is centered on:

Chanting of Psalms

Silent meditation and prayer

Frequent participation in the Eucharist

This form of worship seeks to withdraw from the world to focus purely on God.

Conclusion: The Heart of Worship - Encountering the Divine

Ultimately, Christian worship is not about denominations, rituals, or traditions—it is about encountering God. Whether in a grand cathedral, a house church, or a quiet prayer closet, the essence of worship remains the same:

To lift up the name of God

To experience His presence

To strengthen faith and community

As Jesus told the Samaritan woman in John 4:23-24:

"A time is coming and has now come when the true worshipers will worship the Father in the Spirit and in truth."

From the earliest believers to the present day, Christian worship remains the spiritual lifeblood of the faith—an offering of love, devotion, and surrender to the God who is worthy of all praise.

Angels, Demons, and the Spiritual Realm

Christian views on supernatural beings and spiritual warfare.

From the earliest pages of the Bible to the vivid imagery of Revelation, Christianity has maintained a profound awareness of the unseen spiritual realm. Angels and demons, divine messengers and malevolent forces, play significant roles in the biblical narrative, shaping the cosmic struggle between good and evil.

For many believers, these supernatural beings are not mere mythological constructs but real entities that influence the world in ways both seen and unseen. They are woven into Christian theology, appearing in moments of divine revelation, protection, and temptation. They form the backbone of spiritual warfare, the ongoing battle between God's kingdom and the forces of darkness.

In this section, we will explore the biblical foundations of angels and demons, their roles in Christian thought, and the spiritual battles that define the Christian life.

The Biblical View of Angels

Angels—from the Greek "angelos," meaning "messenger"—are depicted in Scripture as heavenly beings created by God to serve His will. They appear throughout both the Old and New Testaments, often as divine messengers, warriors, or worshipers of God's glory.

1. The Nature and Purpose of Angels

Angels are not physical beings but spiritual entities (Hebrews 1:14), capable of manifesting in human form when necessary. They possess intelligence, emotions, and free will, though they remain steadfast in their allegiance to God.

Their roles include:

Messengers – As seen in Gabriel's annunciation to Mary (Luke 1:26-38).

Warriors – As depicted in Michael leading the armies of heaven (Revelation 12:7).

Guardians – Protecting and ministering to believers (Psalm 91:11, Hebrews 1:14).

Worshipers – Glorifying God continuously (Isaiah 6:2-3, Revelation 4:8-11).

2. Angelic Hierarchy and Orders

Christian tradition, influenced by passages like Colossians 1:16, has proposed a hierarchical order of angels. The most well-known classification comes from Pseudo-Dionysius in the 5th century, who described nine choirs of angels divided into three ranks:

First Sphere (Closest to God):

Seraphim – The highest order, constantly worshiping God (Isaiah 6:2-3).

Cherubim – Guardians of divine mysteries (Genesis 3:24, Ezekiel 10).

Thrones – Represent divine authority and justice (Colossians 1:16).

Second Sphere (Heavenly Governors):

Dominions – Oversee lower angelic ranks.

Virtues – Associated with miracles and strength.

Powers – Warrior angels battling demonic forces.

Third Sphere (Messengers and Protectors):

Principalities – Guardians of nations and rulers.

Archangels – High-ranking messengers, such as Michael and Gabriel.

Angels – The most familiar category, serving as God's messengers and protectors.

Though not explicitly detailed in the Bible, this structure reflects the rich angelology of Christian thought.

The Biblical View of Demons

Just as angels serve God, demons are believed to be fallen angels, rebellious spirits who followed Satan in his defiance against God. They are agents of darkness, working to tempt, deceive, and destroy.

1. The Fall of Satan and His Demons

The origin of Satan is hinted at in passages like Isaiah 14:12-15 and Ezekiel 28:12-17, which describe a powerful being, once full of beauty and wisdom, cast down due to pride.

Revelation 12:7-9 tells of a great battle in heaven, where Michael and his angels fought against Satan (also called Lucifer) and his followers. The rebellious angels were cast out of heaven, becoming the demons who now oppose God's purposes.

"And the great dragon was thrown down, that ancient serpent, who is called the devil and Satan, the deceiver of the whole world—he was thrown down to the earth, and his angels were thrown down with him." (Revelation 12:9)

2. The Role of Demons in Christian Theology

Demons are depicted as spiritual beings that:

Tempt and deceive – Leading humans away from God (Genesis 3:1-5, Matthew 4:1-11).

Cause oppression – Influencing individuals and societies (Mark 5:1-20).

Oppose God's kingdom – Working against the spread of the gospel (Ephesians 6:12).

The New Testament is filled with accounts of Jesus casting out demons, demonstrating His authority over them (Mark 1:21-28, Luke 8:26-39).

Spiritual Warfare: The Battle Between Good and Evil

Christianity teaches that believers are engaged in a spiritual battle—not against flesh and blood, but against "the rulers, the authorities, the powers of this dark world" (Ephesians 6:12).

1. The Armor of God

Paul, in Ephesians 6:10-18, instructs Christians to put on the full armor of God to withstand spiritual attacks:

The Belt of Truth – Standing firm in God's word.

The Breastplate of Righteousness – Living in holiness.

The Gospel of Peace – Proclaiming Christ's message.

The Shield of Faith – Deflecting the lies of the enemy.

The Helmet of Salvation – Confidence in God's saving grace.

The Sword of the Spirit – The Word of God as a weapon.

2. Resisting the Devil

James 4:7 gives a simple but profound strategy:

"Submit yourselves to God. Resist the devil, and he will flee from you."

Spiritual warfare is not about fear but about faith and reliance on God. Through prayer, Scripture, and obedience to God, believers overcome the forces of darkness.

Conclusion: Angels, Demons, and the Christian Life

The reality of angels and demons is not just a theological concept but a daily spiritual reality. Many believers attest to experiences of angelic intervention, demonic oppression, and spiritual battles.

However, Christianity does not teach fear of the unseen but rather confidence in God's sovereignty. As 1 John 4:4 reminds us:

"Greater is He that is in you than he that is in the world."

Angels, as God's messengers, remind us of His constant care. Demons, as deceivers, remind us of the need for vigilance. But ultimately, the victory belongs to Christ, who has triumphed over every force of darkness.

"And having disarmed the powers and authorities, He made a public spectacle of them, triumphing over them by the cross." (Colossians 2:15)

In this battle between light and darkness, the final word has already been spoken: Christ reigns victorious.

Christian Prayer and Devotion

Personal and communal prayer, fasting, and devotion.

Prayer and devotion form the heartbeat of Christian spirituality, a direct line between the human soul and the divine. To pray is to step into the presence of God, to commune with Him in humility, reverence, and faith. Throughout the history of Christianity, prayer has been both a deeply personal experience and a powerful communal practice, shaping individuals and entire faith communities.

From the early church to the present day, prayer has been the foundation of Christian life. Whether whispered in solitude or proclaimed in the grandeur of a cathedral, whether structured through liturgy or uttered in spontaneous conversation, prayer is an expression of faith, hope, and dependence on God.

Alongside prayer, fasting and devotional practices have been crucial elements of Christian piety, serving as disciplines that deepen faith, foster repentance, and draw believers closer to God. In this section, we will explore the different forms of prayer, the role of fasting, and the rich devotional traditions that have shaped Christian worship throughout the centuries.

The Essence of Christian Prayer

At its core, prayer is about relationship. It is not merely a ritual or duty, but an intimate dialogue with the Creator. Jesus himself provided a model for prayer, teaching his disciples how to approach God with both reverence and trust:

"Our Father in heaven, hallowed be your name. Your kingdom come, your will be done, on earth as it is in heaven. Give us today our daily bread. And forgive us our debts, as we also have forgiven our debtors. And lead us not into temptation, but deliver us from the evil one." (Matthew 6:9-13)

This Lord's Prayer, or the "Our Father," encapsulates the major elements of Christian prayer: adoration, submission to God's will, petition, repentance, and spiritual protection.

Types of Prayer in Christianity

Christian prayer takes many forms, each serving a unique purpose in spiritual life.

1. Liturgical and Formal Prayer

Liturgical prayer is structured and often recited in corporate worship settings. These prayers are found in the Mass, the Divine Liturgy, the Anglican Book of Common Prayer, and other Christian traditions. Examples include:

The Lord's Prayer – The most widely recited Christian prayer.

The Psalms – Used in worship and personal meditation.

The Nicene and Apostles' Creeds – Declarations of faith that often accompany prayer.

2. Spontaneous and Conversational Prayer

While many Christians find structured prayers meaningful, others prefer spontaneous prayer, speaking to God in their own words. This form of prayer reflects a personal and immediate connection with God, as seen in the Psalms, where King David cries out in joy, anguish, and thanksgiving.

3. Intercessory Prayer

Intercessory prayer is praying on behalf of others. Christians lift up the needs of their loved ones, their communities, and the world. The Bible encourages this practice:

"I urge, then, first of all, that petitions, prayers, intercession and thanksgiving be made for all people." (1 Timothy 2:1)

Intercessory prayer is central to many Christian traditions, including the Catholic practice of praying to saints to intercede on behalf of believers.

4. Contemplative and Meditative Prayer

Contemplative prayer focuses on stillness, silence, and deep spiritual reflection. This form of prayer has roots in monastic traditions, such as:

Lectio Divina – A slow, meditative reading of Scripture.

The Jesus Prayer – Repeated phrases like "Lord Jesus Christ, Son of God, have mercy on me, a sinner."

Centering Prayer – Focusing on a sacred word to enter a deep state of communion with God.

5. Prayers of Thanksgiving and Praise

Gratitude is a central theme in Christian prayer. Thanksgiving prayers acknowledge God's goodness and provision:

"Give thanks in all circumstances; for this is God's will for you in Christ Jesus." (1 Thessalonians 5:18)

Communal Prayer and Worship

While personal prayer is essential, Christianity places great emphasis on corporate prayer. Jesus said:

"For where two or three gather in my name, there am I with them." (Matthew 18:20)

Throughout history, communal prayer has taken various forms:

1. Prayer in Church Services

Churches across Christian traditions incorporate prayer into their liturgies, including:

Prayers of confession and absolution – Seeking forgiveness for sins.

Prayers of the faithful – Interceding for the needs of the Church and the world.

Eucharistic prayers – Blessing the bread and wine in Communion.

2. Group Prayer and Prayer Meetings

In addition to formal worship, many Christian communities gather for prayer groups, Bible studies, and intercessory meetings. Pentecostal and Charismatic movements, in particular, emphasize spirit-led communal prayer, often accompanied by speaking in tongues and spontaneous expressions of worship.

3. Monastic and Communal Devotion

Monastic communities dedicate themselves to a life of prayer, often following the Liturgy of the Hours, a schedule of prayers recited at set times of the day. The Benedictine, Franciscan, and Eastern Orthodox traditions have preserved these devotional rhythms for centuries.

Fasting as a Spiritual Discipline

Fasting, the practice of abstaining from food for spiritual purposes, has been a part of Christian devotion since biblical times. Jesus himself fasted for 40 days in the wilderness (Matthew 4:2), setting an example for his followers.

Christians fast for various reasons:

To deepen their relationship with God.

As an act of repentance and humility.

To seek divine guidance.

To express solidarity with the poor and suffering.

Forms of Christian Fasting

Lenten Fasting – Practiced in the 40 days leading up to Easter.

Intermittent Fasting – Abstaining from food for specific periods, such as during Holy Week.

Total Fasts – A complete abstention from food for a set time.

Daniel Fasts – A partial fast based on the biblical account of Daniel (Daniel 10:3).

The Catholic Church requires fasting on Ash Wednesday and Good Friday, while Orthodox Christians observe more rigorous fasts, such as the Great Lent and Advent fasts.

The Power of Devotion in Christian Life

Beyond formal prayer and fasting, Christian devotion includes daily acts of faith, such as:

Reading Scripture – Meditating on God's word.

Spiritual journaling – Writing reflections and prayers.

Acts of charity – Expressing faith through love and service.

Pilgrimages – Traveling to sacred sites, such as Jerusalem, Rome, or Lourdes.

For many Christians, devotion is not limited to church services but extends into every aspect of life. As Paul exhorts in 1 Thessalonians 5:17, believers are called to "pray without ceasing", living in constant awareness of God's presence.

Conclusion: The Transformative Power of Prayer

Christian prayer and devotion are not mere rituals but acts of faith that shape the believer's heart and mind. They offer comfort in suffering, strength in weakness, and joy in the presence of God.

Whether through personal prayer, communal worship, fasting, or daily devotion, Christians throughout history have drawn closer to God through these disciplines. As Jesus himself promised:

"Ask, and it will be given to you; seek, and you will find; knock, and the door will be opened to you." (Matthew 7:7)

Through prayer, the door to God's presence is always open.

Christian Ethics and Morality

How Christianity shapes views on life, family, sexuality, and justice.

Ethics lies at the heart of Christianity. From the teachings of Jesus in the Gospels to the moral framework developed by the early Church and later theologians, Christianity has profoundly shaped human understanding of what it means to live a good and righteous life. More than a set of rules, Christian morality is deeply rooted in the character of God—His holiness, love, and justice.

For over two millennia, Christianity has influenced society's perspective on human dignity, family structures, sexuality, justice, and the sanctity of life. It has provided moral guidance for personal conduct and shaped laws, institutions, and cultures worldwide. However, the application of Christian ethics has not been static. As societies evolve, the interpretation and practice of Christian morality continue to be a subject of debate, adaptation, and challenge.

This section will explore the foundations of Christian ethics, how they have shaped views on human life, family, sexuality, and social justice, and the tensions between traditional Christian morality and contemporary societal values.

The Foundations of Christian Ethics

1. The Moral Teachings of Jesus

Christian ethics are most clearly expressed in the life and teachings of Jesus Christ. In contrast to the rigid legalism of the Pharisees, Jesus presented a morality based on love, mercy, and the transformation of the heart. The Sermon on the Mount (Matthew 5-7) remains the most comprehensive ethical discourse in Christianity, emphasizing:

The Beatitudes (Blessed are the poor in spirit, the merciful, the pure in heart, etc.) – Teaching virtues that contrast with worldly values.

Love of neighbor and enemy – Jesus commands His followers to love not only their friends but even their enemies (Matthew 5:44).

The Golden Rule – "Do unto others as you would have them do unto you" (Luke 6:31).

Jesus did not abolish the Mosaic Law, but He reinterpreted it in the light of grace, compassion, and inward transformation rather than mere external compliance. His moral vision was radical, challenging the powerful, uplifting the marginalized, and calling for self-sacrificial love.

2. The Role of Scripture in Christian Ethics

Christian morality is biblically grounded, drawing principles from both the Old and New Testaments. While the Old Testament provides the foundation for justice, social order, and divine law (e.g., the Ten Commandments), the New Testament focuses on grace, love, and the fulfillment of the Law through Christ.

The Decalogue (Ten Commandments) – Forms the bedrock of Christian ethics, emphasizing honesty, fidelity, respect for life, and reverence for God.

Pauline Ethics – The letters of St. Paul (Romans, Corinthians, Galatians) offer moral guidance on sexuality, family roles, and Christian conduct in a pagan society.

Scripture is not just a rulebook; it offers principles that help Christians navigate modern moral dilemmas in areas such as medical ethics, politics, and personal conduct.

Christian Views on Human Life and Dignity

Christianity teaches that human life is sacred, created in the image of God (imago Dei) (Genesis 1:27). This belief has profound ethical implications:

1. The Sanctity of Life

Christianity upholds the intrinsic worth of every human being, from conception to natural death. This has influenced Christian positions on:

Abortion – Generally opposed by the Catholic Church and many Protestant denominations, based on the belief that life begins at conception (Psalm 139:13-16).

Euthanasia – Considered morally wrong, as life is a gift from God and suffering has spiritual meaning (Job 1:21).

Capital Punishment – Historically accepted but increasingly debated, with many Christians advocating for mercy over retribution.

2. The Concept of Human Rights

Christian ethics has played a pivotal role in the development of human rights, including:

The abolition of slavery (inspired by Galatians 3:28).

The dignity of the poor and marginalized (Matthew 25:40).

The push for social justice and human equality.

Christian Views on Family and Marriage

The family is central to Christian morality, seen as a reflection of God's relationship with His people. The Bible presents marriage as a covenant between a man and a woman (Genesis 2:24), and it places great emphasis on the responsibilities of spouses, parents, and children.

1. Marriage as a Sacred Institution

Christianity teaches that marriage is:

Monogamous – Reflecting Christ's relationship with the Church (Ephesians 5:22-33).

Lifelong – Divorce is discouraged, though views vary (Matthew 19:6).

Rooted in love and mutual sacrifice – "Husbands, love your wives as Christ loved the Church" (Ephesians 5:25).

2. Parenting and Family Roles

Christian ethics emphasize the responsibility of parents to raise children in faith:

"Train up a child in the way he should go" (Proverbs 22:6).

The role of fathers and mothers as spiritual guides and moral examples.

Many Christian traditions promote gender complementarity, though modern debates question traditional roles and emphasize equality in marriage.

Christian Views on Sexuality

Sexuality in Christian ethics is seen as a sacred gift, meant to be expressed within the boundaries of marriage. Key teachings include:

Chastity – Sexual purity before marriage.

Faithfulness – Adultery is condemned (Exodus 20:14).

Homosexuality – A complex and debated issue; traditional Christian teaching sees marriage as between a man and a woman, while some modern denominations affirm LGBTQ+ inclusion.

Christian views on sexuality are often countercultural, creating tensions in secular societies that embrace sexual autonomy.

Christian Ethics and Social Justice

Christianity has been a driving force in the pursuit of justice, advocating for the poor, oppressed, and disenfranchised.

1. Care for the Poor and Oppressed

Jesus identifies with the poor: "Whatever you did for the least of these, you did for me" (Matthew 25:40).

The early Church practiced radical generosity, pooling resources to help those in need (Acts 2:44-45).

Many Christian organizations today lead charitable efforts, hospitals, and humanitarian missions.

2. Justice and the Common Good

Christianity promotes fairness, honesty, and peace in governance.

Many abolitionists, civil rights activists, and reformers (e.g., William Wilberforce, Martin Luther King Jr.) were driven by Christian ethics.

The Challenge of Christian Ethics in a Secular World

While Christian morality has shaped Western civilization, modern secularism has challenged many traditional Christian values. Topics like abortion, LGBTQ+ rights, gender roles, and religious liberty remain highly debated.

Some see Christian ethics as a moral anchor, while others view it as restrictive. However, Christianity continues to offer a moral framework rooted in love, justice, and human dignity, guiding millions in their personal and public lives.

Conclusion: The Enduring Influence of Christian Morality

Christian ethics is not merely a set of rules; it is a call to holiness, love, and service. Rooted in the teachings of Christ, Scripture, and Church tradition, Christian morality challenges believers to live with integrity, treat others with dignity, and seek justice in an often unjust world.

Even as societal norms shift, the ethical principles of Christianity remain a source of guidance, hope, and moral courage for those who seek to live by faith in a complex world.

✝ Christian Festivals and Holy Days

Christmas, Easter, Pentecost, and other significant celebrations.

Throughout its long history, Christianity has developed a rich tapestry of festivals and holy days that commemorate key events in the life of Jesus Christ, the early Church, and the saints. These celebrations serve as moments of spiritual reflection, communal worship, and deep theological significance, marking the rhythm of the Christian calendar.

Some of these holy days—like Christmas and Easter—are well known even outside of Christian communities. Others, like Pentecost, Epiphany, and Lent, hold immense importance within the Church but are less recognized in secular culture. Christian festivals are not merely historical commemorations; they are moments when believers engage with the mysteries of their faith and reenact the great events of salvation history.

This chapter explores the major Christian celebrations, their historical roots, their theological meaning, and how they are observed across different traditions.

Christmas: The Celebration of Christ's Birth

Christmas is perhaps the most widely recognized Christian festival, celebrated on December 25th by most Western churches and on January 7th by many Eastern Orthodox traditions (due to differences in the Gregorian and Julian calendars).

1. The Biblical and Theological Meaning of Christmas

Christmas commemorates the birth of Jesus Christ in Bethlehem, an event recorded in the Gospels of Matthew and Luke. Theologically, it is the Incarnation—God becoming flesh (John 1:14), a moment when the divine entered human history in the most vulnerable form: as a baby.

Key biblical themes associated with Christmas include:

Fulfillment of prophecy – Jesus' birth fulfills Old Testament promises (Isaiah 7:14, Micah 5:2).

Salvation and redemption – The birth of Christ is the beginning of God's redemptive work.

Divine humility – God chose to be born in a manger rather than a palace, emphasizing humility and love.

2. The History of Christmas Traditions

The Nativity Scene (Crèche) – Originated with St. Francis of Assisi in the 13th century.

The Christmas Tree – A tradition with medieval roots, symbolizing eternal life.

Gift-Giving – Reflects the gifts of the Magi (Matthew 2:11) and the generosity of St. Nicholas, the inspiration for Santa Claus.

Many Christian denominations observe Advent—the four weeks leading up to Christmas—as a time of preparation, fasting, and reflection on Christ's coming.

Easter: The Resurrection of Christ

If Christmas celebrates Christ's arrival, Easter celebrates His victory—His triumph over sin and death through the Resurrection. Easter is the oldest and most important Christian festival, observed on the first Sunday after the first full moon following the spring equinox (a calculation that places it between March 22nd and April 25th).

1. The Biblical and Theological Meaning of Easter

Easter marks the Resurrection of Jesus three days after His crucifixion, as recorded in all four Gospels. It is the heart of Christian faith because:

It confirms Jesus' divinity – "If Christ has not been raised, your faith is futile" (1 Corinthians 15:17).

It secures salvation – Through His Resurrection, Jesus conquers sin and death.

It promises eternal life – The Resurrection is the foundation of Christian hope in life after death.

2. The Holy Week: The Journey to Easter

Easter is the climax of Holy Week, which reenacts the final days of Jesus' earthly life:

Palm Sunday – Jesus' triumphant entry into Jerusalem.

Maundy Thursday – The Last Supper, where Jesus institutes the Eucharist.

Good Friday – The Crucifixion, marked by sorrowful reflection and fasting.

Holy Saturday – A day of waiting, symbolizing Jesus' time in the tomb.

3. Easter Traditions and Symbols

The Easter Vigil – A dramatic Saturday night service, celebrating Christ's passage from death to life.

The Empty Tomb – Central to Easter imagery, symbolizing Christ's victory over death.

Easter Eggs – Symbolize new life and Christ's Resurrection.

The season of Lent precedes Easter—a 40-day period of fasting, repentance, and spiritual preparation, mirroring Jesus' 40 days in the wilderness.

Pentecost: The Birth of the Church

Fifty days after Easter, Christians celebrate Pentecost, the day the Holy Spirit descended upon the Apostles in Jerusalem, as described in Acts 2.

1. The Biblical and Theological Meaning of Pentecost

Pentecost marks the beginning of the Church, when the Apostles, filled with the Holy Spirit, boldly preached the Gospel and baptized thousands. It highlights:

The fulfillment of Jesus' promise to send the Holy Spirit (John

14:16).

The empowerment of believers to spread the Gospel.

The universality of salvation – The Apostles speak in different tongues, symbolizing Christianity's mission to all nations.

2. Pentecost Traditions

Red vestments – Symbolizing the fire of the Holy Spirit.

Confirmation ceremonies – In some traditions, Pentecost is associated with confirming believers in faith.

Vigils and prayers for renewal – Many churches pray for a fresh outpouring of the Holy Spirit.

Other Major Christian Celebrations

1. Epiphany (January 6th)

Celebrates the visit of the Magi (in Western Christianity) and Jesus' baptism (in Eastern traditions). It emphasizes:

Jesus as King and Savior for all nations (symbolized by the Magi).

The revelation of Christ to the world (Greek: epiphaneia, meaning "appearance").

2. Ascension Day (40 Days After Easter)

Marks Christ's ascension into heaven (Acts 1:9-11). It affirms:

Jesus' exaltation as Lord of all.

The promise of His return in the Second Coming.

3. All Saints' Day (November 1st)

Honors all holy men and women throughout history who have lived faithful lives. It is followed by All Souls' Day (November 2nd), when prayers are offered for the deceased.

4. Feast Days of Saints

Different Christian traditions commemorate various saints and martyrs, such as:

St. Patrick's Day (March 17th) – Honoring the missionary who brought Christianity to Ireland.

St. Francis of Assisi (October 4th) – Patron of animals and nature.

The Christian Calendar: A Cycle of Redemption

The Christian liturgical calendar is structured around these holy days, forming a sacred rhythm that guides believers through the life of Christ and the story of salvation.

1. The Liturgical Seasons

Advent – A time of preparation before Christmas.

Lent – A period of fasting before Easter.

Ordinary Time – The weeks between major celebrations, focusing on discipleship.

Each season deepens the spiritual life of the believer, connecting them to the mystery of faith.

Conclusion: The Meaning Behind the Celebrations

Christian festivals are not merely historical commemorations; they are acts of worship, spiritual renewal, and communal faith. They connect believers across centuries and cultures, reminding them of God's ongoing work in human history.

Whether through joyous feasts like Christmas, solemn reflections like Good Friday, or the empowering outpouring of Pentecost, Christian holy days continue to shape the identity, faith, and devotion of believers worldwide.

Christian Missions and Evangelism

The Great Commission and the role of missionaries.

From its very inception, Christianity has been a faith rooted in proclamation and outreach. At the heart of Christian identity lies a mandate given by Jesus Himself—the Great Commission—a command that has propelled generations of believers across continents, languages, and cultures to spread the message of Christ.

Christian missions and evangelism are not merely historical phenomena; they continue to shape the global religious landscape today. Whether through the dedicated lives of early apostles, medieval missionaries braving unknown lands, or modern evangelists utilizing digital platforms, the Christian faith has always been one of expansion, invitation, and transformation.

This chapter explores the theological foundation of missions, the historical development of evangelism, and the ongoing impact of Christian outreach in the modern world.

The Great Commission: Christ's Command to Evangelize

Before His ascension into heaven, Jesus gave His disciples a final instruction, one that would define the mission of the Church for centuries to come. This passage, known as the Great Commission, is found in Matthew 28:18-20:

"Go therefore and make disciples of all nations, baptizing them in the name of the Father and of the Son and of the Holy Spirit, teaching them to observe all that I have commanded you. And behold, I am with you always, to the end of the age."

This command highlights several key aspects of Christian missions:

A Universal Scope – The Gospel is not restricted to a single people or nation; it is for "all nations."

The Call to Discipleship – Evangelism is not just about conversion but about forming devoted followers of Christ.

Baptism and Teaching – Mission work involves both initiation into the faith (baptism) and spiritual growth (teaching the commandments of Christ).

Christ's Presence – Missionaries do not act alone; they carry the presence and authority of Jesus wherever they go.

This Great Commission laid the groundwork for every missionary movement, from the apostolic era to the present day.

The Early Christian Missionaries: The Apostles and the Expansion of the Faith

The earliest Christian mission work was undertaken by Jesus' own disciples, who, empowered by the Holy Spirit at Pentecost (Acts 2), set out to proclaim Christ to the world.

1. Paul: The Missionary to the Gentiles

No figure looms larger in early Christian missions than the Apostle Paul. Formerly a persecutor of Christians, Paul underwent a dramatic conversion and became the faith's most tireless missionary. His missionary journeys took him through:

Asia Minor (modern-day Turkey)

Greece and Rome

The islands of the Mediterranean

Paul's strategy was both bold and methodical:

He preached first in synagogues, reaching Jews familiar with the Scriptures.

He engaged with Gentiles, using their cultural and philosophical frameworks to point them to Christ.

He established churches and appointed leaders, ensuring the

continuity of his work.

His letters (epistles), many of which are now part of the New Testament, were a form of missionary follow-up, strengthening new believers and instructing them in the faith.

2. The Apostolic Expansion Beyond the Roman Empire

Thomas is said to have traveled to India, planting Christian communities that still exist today.

Mark is traditionally credited with founding the Church in Egypt.

Peter and others carried the faith to Rome and beyond.

By the end of the first century, Christianity had reached North Africa, Europe, and Asia, despite fierce persecution by Roman authorities.

Medieval and Early Modern Missions: The Christianization of Europe and Beyond

1. The Spread of Christianity in Europe

During the early medieval period, Christianity spread across the Germanic and Slavic lands, largely due to the work of monastic missionaries like:

St. Patrick (Ireland) – Converted the Irish and established monasteries.

St. Augustine of Canterbury (England) – Evangelized the Anglo-Saxons.

Cyril and Methodius (Slavic regions) – Developed the Cyrillic alphabet to translate Scripture.

By the 10th century, Christianity had become the dominant faith in Europe.

2. The Age of Exploration and Missions

As European nations explored new territories, Christian missionaries traveled alongside them. This era saw both incredible dedication and troubling coercion, as missionary work was often linked to colonial expansion.

Notable missionary movements include:

The Jesuits (16th century) – A Catholic order that evangelized Asia, Africa, and the Americas.

Francis Xavier – One of the first missionaries to reach Japan and India.

Protestant Missions (18th-19th century) – Figures like William Carey (India) and David Livingstone (Africa) sought to spread Christianity without colonial rule.

Despite the complicated legacy of missions in the colonial period, these efforts planted churches worldwide, many of which remain strong today.

Modern Evangelism: The Global Church and New Frontiers

1. The Rise of Evangelical and Pentecostal Missions

The 20th and 21st centuries saw a massive rise in evangelical and Pentecostal missionary work, often led by:

Independent missionaries

Mega-church organizations

Television and digital evangelism

Pentecostalism, with its emphasis on spiritual gifts and personal experience, has fueled rapid church growth in Africa, Latin America, and Asia.

2. Mission Work in the Secular and Islamic World

Christian missions today face unique challenges:

In secular societies, faith is often seen as irrelevant.

In Islamic nations, evangelism is restricted, and missionaries risk persecution.

Despite this, underground churches and digital ministries continue to grow in China, Iran, and the Middle East.

Conclusion: The Enduring Call to Evangelize

Christian missions and evangelism are as vital today as they were in the first century. The Great Commission remains an ongoing command, one that has:

Transformed civilizations

Empowered millions of believers

Continued to spread the message of hope and redemption

While methods have changed—moving from oral preaching to digital evangelism—the message remains the same: Christ's call to go and make disciples of all nations.

Monasticism and Religious Orders

The history and purpose of monks, nuns, and religious communities.

Throughout the centuries, Christianity has taken on many forms of devotion, practice, and community life, but few have been as enduring and transformative as monasticism. The monastic tradition, which has given rise to some of the most profound spiritual movements in Christian history, began as a radical pursuit of holiness—one that sought to renounce the distractions of the world in favor of a life devoted to prayer, contemplation, and service.

The monastic impulse has driven men and women to forsake personal wealth, political ambition, and even family ties in order to live in complete dedication to God. Monks, nuns, and religious communities have played a pivotal role in shaping Christian thought, preserving sacred texts, and even influencing art, education, and social justice.

This chapter will explore the origins of Christian monasticism, the development of religious orders, and the enduring purpose of these communities in today's world.

The Birth of Christian Monasticism: From the Desert Fathers to Organized Communities

1. The Desert Fathers and the Call to Solitude

The origins of Christian monasticism can be traced to the early centuries of Christianity, when devout men and women withdrew into the deserts of Egypt and Syria to seek a life of prayer and asceticism. Known as the Desert Fathers and Mothers, these individuals renounced worldly attachments in an effort to grow closer to God.

Among the most famous of these early monks was St. Anthony the

Great (251-356 AD), an Egyptian ascetic who is often regarded as the father of Christian monasticism. Inspired by Jesus' command to the rich young ruler—"Go, sell what you own and give to the poor, and you will have treasure in heaven" (Mark 10:21)—Anthony abandoned his wealth and retreated into the wilderness.

Others soon followed his example, forming small hermitic communities, living in prayer and self-denial. These monks, though living in solitude, developed a system of spiritual mentorship, sharing their wisdom with those who sought guidance. Their sayings and writings were collected into texts like The Sayings of the Desert Fathers, which continue to inspire monastics and spiritual seekers today.

2. The Rise of Organized Monasticism: St. Pachomius and St. Benedict

While the early monks lived as hermits, monasticism soon took a more structured and communal form. One of the key figures in this transition was St. Pachomius (292-348 AD), who established the first formal monastic communities in Egypt. His monasteries provided a structured rule of life, emphasizing prayer, work, and communal living.

A few centuries later, St. Benedict of Nursia (480-547 AD) revolutionized Western monasticism by creating the Rule of St. Benedict, a guidebook for monastic life that balanced prayer, work (labor), and study. His monasteries became centers of education, agriculture, and manuscript preservation, ensuring that Christianity and classical learning survived even as the Roman Empire collapsed.

Benedictine monasticism laid the foundation for many religious orders that followed, inspiring monks and nuns across Europe.

The Growth of Religious Orders: The Diversity of Monastic Life

As Christianity spread and evolved, different monastic orders emerged, each emphasizing a unique aspect of Christian devotion.

1. The Benedictines: "Ora et Labora" (Pray and Work)

Founded by St. Benedict, the Benedictines focused on prayer, work, and stability. Their monasteries became self-sufficient communities, with monks engaged in farming, copying manuscripts, and theological study. The famous Benedictine monasteries of Europe, such as Monte Cassino, became intellectual and cultural hubs.

2. The Cistercians and Trappists: A Return to Simplicity

In the 12th century, the Cistercians sought to reform Benedictine monasticism by emphasizing greater simplicity, manual labor, and strict discipline. The Trappists, a later offshoot, practiced even greater austerity, observing silence and rigorous self-denial.

3. The Mendicant Orders: Preaching to the People

Unlike traditional monastic orders that remained in cloistered settings, the mendicant orders took monasticism into the streets, preaching directly to the people.

The Franciscans (Founded by St. Francis of Assisi, 1209 AD): Devoted to poverty, simplicity, and service to the poor.

The Dominicans (Founded by St. Dominic, 1216 AD): Focused on preaching and intellectual life, combating heresy through scholarship.

Both orders played a key role in evangelization, education, and missions.

4. The Jesuits: The Intellectual Missionaries

Founded in 1540 by St. Ignatius of Loyola, the Jesuits (Society of Jesus) emphasized education, missionary work, and intellectual rigor. They established schools and universities around the world, including some of the most prestigious institutions in the modern era.

The Purpose of Monastic Life: Why Monks and Nuns Matter

Many wonder: Why do people choose monastic life? What is the significance of monks and nuns withdrawing from the world?

A Life Devoted to God – Monks and nuns renounce earthly distractions to focus entirely on prayer, meditation, and communion with God.

Spiritual Discipline – Monasticism cultivates virtues such as humility, patience, and self-control, modeling an alternative way of Christian living.

Service to Society – Monastic communities have long been centers of learning, charity, and hospitality. They run hospitals, schools, and orphanages.

Guardians of Christian Tradition – Monks preserved sacred texts and theological knowledge, ensuring the survival of Christianity through history.

Even in the modern world, monastic communities remain places of spiritual retreat, welcoming those who seek deeper faith.

Monasticism in the Modern Age: Relevance and Challenges

Though monastic life has declined in the modern era, it remains a powerful witness to Christian spirituality.

Monastic Retreats – Many monasteries now offer retreat programs where laypeople can experience silence, prayer, and renewal.

New Monasticism – Some Christian groups, even outside Catholic and Orthodox traditions, have adopted monastic-style living in urban settings.

Continued Service – Monastic communities still run hospitals, teach, and provide humanitarian aid across the globe.

However, monasteries face challenges as fewer young people choose religious life. Still, the impact of monks and nuns endures in Christian thought, service, and contemplation.

Conclusion: The Lasting Legacy of Monasticism

For nearly two millennia, monks, nuns, and religious orders have shaped Christianity, preserving its teachings, serving the poor, and offering a model of radical devotion.

Whether in desert solitude, medieval scriptoria, or modern cities, the monastic call remains the same: a life fully given to prayer, discipline, and love for God. While the world changes, the monastic spirit endures, continuing to inspire generations of seekers who long for something more than the distractions of daily life—a life fully centered on Christ.

✝ Roman Catholicism
Doctrine, structure, and key differences from Protestantism.

Roman Catholicism, the largest branch of Christianity, stands as one of the most enduring and influential religious traditions in history. With over 1.3 billion adherents worldwide, the Catholic Church has shaped the spiritual, cultural, and political landscapes of nations for centuries. Rooted in apostolic succession, upheld by a hierarchical structure, and guided by a rich theological tradition, Catholicism presents a distinctive vision of Christian life that sets it apart from Protestantism and other Christian movements.

This section explores the core doctrines of Catholicism, the structure of the Church, and its key differences from Protestantism, shedding light on the enduring significance of this ancient tradition.

The Foundations of Catholic Doctrine

At the heart of Roman Catholic belief is the conviction that the Church, founded by Jesus Christ and entrusted to the apostles, is the true and authoritative institution for interpreting Scripture and guiding the faithful. This authority is rooted in Sacred Tradition and Sacred Scripture, both of which are viewed as complementary sources of divine revelation.

1. The Magisterium: The Teaching Authority of the Church

One of the defining aspects of Catholicism is the Magisterium, the Church's teaching authority, which resides in the Pope and the bishops in communion with him. This authority ensures the preservation of doctrinal truth and provides authoritative interpretations of Scripture and Tradition. Unlike Protestantism, which generally emphasizes individual interpretation of the Bible, Catholicism insists on a centralized and continuous tradition of interpretation dating back to the apostles.

2. The Sacraments: Channels of Divine Grace

A crucial element of Catholic theology is its sacramental system. The Catholic Church recognizes seven sacraments, which are considered visible signs of God's grace:

Baptism – The initiation into the Christian faith.

Eucharist (Holy Communion) – The reception of Christ's body and blood.

Confirmation – The strengthening of faith through the Holy Spirit.

Reconciliation (Confession) – The forgiveness of sins through a priest.

Anointing of the Sick – Healing and grace for the ill or dying.

Holy Orders – The ordination of priests and bishops.

Matrimony – The sacred union of husband and wife.

These sacraments are not merely symbolic; they are seen as actual means of divine grace, distinguishing Catholic practice from Protestant traditions that often emphasize sacraments as memorials or symbolic acts rather than spiritual transformations.

3. The Eucharist and Transubstantiation

One of the most significant theological distinctions between Catholicism and Protestantism concerns the Eucharist. The Catholic Church teaches the doctrine of Transubstantiation, meaning that during the Mass, the bread and wine used in Communion become the actual body and blood of Christ, though their outward appearance remains unchanged. This contrasts sharply with most Protestant denominations, which either view Communion as symbolic or believe in a spiritual presence of Christ rather than a physical transformation.

4. The Role of Mary and the Saints

Catholic devotion to Mary, the Mother of God, and the saints is another distinctive feature. Catholics believe that Mary holds a special place in salvation history and venerate her through doctrines such as the Immaculate Conception (her being conceived without sin) and the Assumption (her being taken body and soul into heaven).

Likewise, Catholics pray to saints as intercessors who bring prayers before God, believing that the Communion of Saints unites believers across time and space. While Protestants emphasize a direct relationship with God, Catholicism maintains that prayers to saints enhance this relationship rather than replace it.

5. Purgatory and the Afterlife

Catholic eschatology includes the doctrine of Purgatory, a state of purification for souls who die in grace but still require cleansing from sin before entering heaven. This belief in a post-death purification process is absent in most Protestant theology, which tends to emphasize immediate entry into either heaven or hell upon death.

The Structure of the Catholic Church

The Catholic Church is highly hierarchical, with a centralized authority in Rome.

The Pope – The Bishop of Rome, regarded as the Successor of St. Peter, is the supreme leader of the Catholic Church.

Cardinals – High-ranking clergy who serve as advisors to the Pope and elect his successor.

Bishops – Overseers of dioceses, responsible for teaching, governance, and pastoral care.

Priests – Ordained ministers who lead local parishes and administer the sacraments.

Deacons – Assistants to priests, serving in charity, preaching, and liturgical functions.

This structured authority ensures unity in doctrine and practice, in contrast to Protestantism, which is often more decentralized and diverse in governance.

Key Differences Between Catholicism and Protestantism

While both traditions share a belief in Jesus Christ, the Bible, and salvation, they differ significantly in authority, doctrine, and practice.

Aspect	Roman Catholicism	Protestantism
Authority	Magisterium (Pope and bishops)	Sola Scriptura (Bible alone)
Sacraments	Seven sacraments	Usually two (Baptism, Eucharist)
Eucharist	Transubstantiation (Real Presence)	Symbolic or spiritual presence
Mary and Saints	Venerated, intercessors	Generally not venerated
Salvation	Faith and works	Faith alone (Sola Fide)
Purgatory	Belief in purification after death	Generally rejected
Church Leadership	Pope and hierarchy	No central authority

Conclusion: The Enduring Legacy of Catholicism

For over 2,000 years, Catholicism has preserved Christian tradition, shaped Western civilization, and remained a spiritual home for millions. Its influence is seen in theology, art, music, education, and humanitarian efforts worldwide.

Despite challenges such as secularization, theological disputes, and internal reforms, the Catholic Church continues to be a powerful force in global Christianity. Whether through its liturgical beauty, sacramental depth, or historical continuity, Catholicism stands as a testament to the enduring search for divine truth—one that continues to shape faith, culture, and history.

Eastern Orthodoxy

Theology, liturgy, and key distinctions from Western Christianity.

Eastern Orthodoxy is one of the three main branches of Christianity, alongside Roman Catholicism and Protestantism. It is the dominant Christian tradition in Eastern Europe, Russia, and parts of the Middle East, tracing its lineage back to the earliest days of Christianity. With a theological framework deeply rooted in the Church Fathers, mystical spirituality, and elaborate liturgical tradition, Orthodoxy has preserved a distinct form of Christianity that sets it apart from the Catholic and Protestant traditions of the West.

This section explores the theological foundations, liturgical practices, and key distinctions that define Eastern Orthodoxy and how it has maintained its unique identity for over a millennium.

Theology of Eastern Orthodoxy

The theology of the Orthodox Church is deeply mystical, emphasizing participation in God, communal worship, and the transformation of the believer. Unlike Western Christianity, which often employs systematic theology and scholastic reasoning, Orthodoxy leans toward an experiential and mystical approach to understanding divine truths.

1. Theosis: The Goal of Salvation

One of the most distinctive aspects of Orthodox theology is the doctrine of theosis—the belief that the goal of human life is to become united with God. This process of divinization is made possible through prayer, fasting, sacraments, and ascetic practices. Unlike the Catholic and Protestant emphasis on legal atonement and justification, theosis sees salvation as an ongoing journey of transformation into the likeness of Christ.

2. Sacred Tradition and Apostolic Continuity

The Orthodox Church holds that Sacred Tradition is the foundation of Christian faith, equal in authority to Scripture. This includes the writings of the Church Fathers, the decisions of the Ecumenical Councils, and the liturgical and mystical traditions passed down through centuries.

Unlike Protestantism, which upholds Sola Scriptura (Scripture alone), the Orthodox tradition asserts that the Bible must be interpreted within the living tradition of the Church. The authority of the Church is maintained through apostolic succession, ensuring that bishops today stand in direct continuity with the apostles.

3. The Holy Trinity: The Filioque Controversy

Both Eastern Orthodoxy and Roman Catholicism affirm belief in the Holy Trinity—Father, Son, and Holy Spirit—but they differ in how they understand the procession of the Holy Spirit.

In the Nicene Creed, Orthodox Christians state that the Holy Spirit proceeds from the Father.

In Western Christianity, the Catholic Church later added "and the Son" (Filioque), asserting that the Spirit proceeds from both the Father and the Son.

This theological difference became a major point of contention between Eastern and Western Christianity, contributing to the Great Schism of 1054.

Liturgy and Worship in Eastern Orthodoxy

One of the most striking features of Orthodoxy is its deeply reverential and symbolic worship, which aims to reflect the divine reality of heaven on earth.

1. The Divine Liturgy

Orthodox services are known for their majestic beauty, elaborate chanting, and deep symbolism. The main service, called the Divine Liturgy, follows a structure largely unchanged since the early Church.

The Liturgy of St. John Chrysostom is the most commonly used, featuring prayers, hymns, incense, and a focus on the mystery of the Eucharist.

The Liturgy of St. Basil the Great is used on special feast days and retains longer, more theological prayers.

Unlike Western Christianity, which has seen varied worship styles develop over time, Orthodoxy insists on preserving its ancient liturgical forms.

2. Icons and Sacred Art

Icons (holy images of Christ, Mary, and the saints) play a central role in Orthodox worship. Unlike Western Christian art, which often aims for realism, Orthodox icons are highly stylized, meant to convey spiritual truths rather than physical likeness.

Veneration of icons (not worship) is seen as a way to honor the presence of Christ and the saints in the Church.

The Iconostasis, a screen covered in icons, separates the sanctuary from the congregation, symbolizing the mystery of heaven.

3. Chanting and the Absence of Instruments

In Orthodox churches, music is exclusively vocal—no instruments are used. The chanting, which varies across Greek, Russian, and other traditions, is meant to elevate the soul to God. This differs from Western Christianity, where organs, pianos, and modern instruments are often used in worship.

4. Fasting and Asceticism

Orthodox Christians observe rigorous fasting traditions, with nearly half the year designated as periods of dietary restrictions and spiritual discipline. The most significant fasting period is Great Lent, a 40-day preparation for Easter that involves abstaining from meat, dairy, and other foods. This emphasis on asceticism is less prominent in many Western Christian traditions.

Key Distinctions Between Eastern Orthodoxy and Western Christianity

While Eastern Orthodoxy shares foundational Christian beliefs with Catholicism and Protestantism, there are major theological, liturgical, and cultural differences.

Aspect	Eastern Orthodoxy	Roman Catholicism	Protestantism
Authority	Sacred Tradition and the Ecumenical Councils	Pope as supreme authority	Sola Scriptura (Bible alone)
Salvation	Theosis (union with God)	Justification through faith and works	Justification by faith alone
Eucharist	Mystery, real presence of Christ	Transubstantiation	Symbolic or spiritual presence
Holy Spirit	Proceeds from the Father only	Proceeds from the Father and the Son (Filioque)	Varies by denomination
Clergy	Married priests allowed, but bishops must be celibate	Priestly celibacy required	Generally no celibacy requirement
Worship Style	Highly liturgical, incense, chanting, icons	Liturgical with more diversity	Varies widely, from formal to contemporary
Purgatory	Rejected, but prayers for the dead encouraged	Belief in purgatory as purification	Generally rejected
Fasting and Asceticism	Strict fasting seasons	Moderate fasting traditions	Less emphasis on fasting

Conclusion: The Enduring Legacy of Eastern Orthodoxy

Eastern Orthodoxy has remained remarkably unchanged in its theology and liturgical practice for over 1,000 years. Despite persecutions under the Ottoman Empire, Soviet communism, and secular modernity, the Orthodox Church has maintained a strong spiritual and cultural identity.

Today, Orthodoxy continues to thrive in Eastern Europe, Greece, Russia, and growing communities in the West, attracting those who seek a mystical, traditional, and deeply historical form of Christianity.

With its rich liturgical beauty, emphasis on divine mystery, and continuity with the early Church, Eastern Orthodoxy remains a profound expression of Christian faith, offering a distinctive path to encountering God through worship, tradition, and spiritual transformation.

Protestantism and Its Branches

Lutheranism, Calvinism, Baptists, Methodists, and others.

Protestantism is one of the three major branches of Christianity, alongside Roman Catholicism and Eastern Orthodoxy. It emerged in the 16th century Reformation, a religious movement that sought to reform perceived errors and corruptions within the Catholic Church. Led by figures such as Martin Luther, John Calvin, and Huldrych Zwingli, Protestantism developed into a diverse tradition encompassing many theological interpretations, worship styles, and church structures.

Unlike Catholicism and Orthodoxy, which emphasize tradition and hierarchical authority, Protestantism is characterized by individual interpretation of Scripture, salvation by faith alone, and a rejection of papal authority. Over time, numerous Protestant denominations emerged, each with its own doctrinal emphases. This section will explore the major branches of Protestantism, their theological distinctives, and their impact on global Christianity.

Origins of Protestantism

The Protestant Reformation began in 1517 when Martin Luther, a German monk and theologian, nailed his Ninety-Five Theses to the church door in Wittenberg. He protested against the sale of indulgences (payments for the forgiveness of sins) and called for a return to biblical authority. His movement quickly spread across Germany and beyond, leading to schisms within Christendom.

Other reformers, such as John Calvin in Switzerland and Huldrych Zwingli, contributed to the development of distinct theological perspectives. By the 17th century, Protestantism had diversified into several major branches, including Lutheranism, Calvinism (Reformed Tradition), Anglicanism, and the Radical Reformation (which produced groups such as the Anabaptists and Baptists).

Key Protestant Doctrines

While Protestant denominations vary in their beliefs, they generally share a few core doctrines:

Sola Scriptura ("Scripture Alone") – The belief that the Bible is the highest authority in matters of faith and doctrine, rejecting the Catholic view that Sacred Tradition holds equal weight.

Sola Fide ("Faith Alone") – The teaching that salvation comes through faith in Jesus Christ alone, rather than a combination of faith and works.

Sola Gratia ("Grace Alone") – The belief that salvation is a free gift from God, not earned by human effort.

The Priesthood of All Believers – The idea that all Christians have direct access to God, without the need for a hierarchical priesthood.

Despite these commonalities, Protestantism is not a monolithic movement—its branches developed different interpretations of theology, governance, and worship.

Major Branches of Protestantism

1. Lutheranism

Founder: Martin Luther (1483–1546)

Main Beliefs: Justification by faith, two sacraments (Baptism and the Lord's Supper), Christ's real presence in the Eucharist.

Key Texts: Augsburg Confession (1530), Small and Large Catechisms of Luther.

Lutheranism was the first Protestant movement and remains one of the largest Protestant traditions today, with strong followings in Germany, Scandinavia, and the United States. It emphasizes salvation by faith alone (justification), the authority of Scripture, and the importance of liturgical worship.

Lutherans reject the Catholic belief in transubstantiation (the bread and wine becoming the literal body and blood of Christ) but affirm a real, spiritual presence of Christ in the Eucharist. The movement is divided into several branches, including the Evangelical Lutheran Church in America (ELCA) and the Lutheran Church—Missouri Synod (LCMS).

2. Calvinism (Reformed Tradition)

Founder: John Calvin (1509-1564)

Main Beliefs: Predestination, the sovereignty of God, covenant theology.

Key Texts: The Institutes of the Christian Religion (1536).

Calvinism, also known as the Reformed Tradition, arose from John Calvin's teachings in Geneva, Switzerland. It became one of the most influential Protestant traditions, especially in Scotland, the Netherlands, and parts of the United States.

Calvinists emphasize God's absolute sovereignty, teaching predestination—the belief that God has chosen certain individuals for salvation before the foundation of the world. They also stress a disciplined Christian life, simple worship, and a rejection of elaborate rituals.

Calvinism gave rise to Presbyterianism (led by John Knox in Scotland) and influenced movements such as the Puritans in England and the Dutch Reformed Church.

3. Anglicanism

Founder: King Henry VIII (1491-1547)

Main Beliefs: Middle way between Catholicism and Protestantism, apostolic succession, use of the Book of Common Prayer.

Key Texts: The Thirty-Nine Articles, The Book of Common Prayer.

Anglicanism originated in England when King Henry VIII broke from the Catholic Church in 1534 over the Pope's refusal to annul his marriage. Over time, the Anglican Church developed its own theological identity, combining Protestant doctrine with Catholic traditions.

The Church of England and its global counterpart, the Anglican Communion, emphasize liturgical worship, the authority of bishops, and a balance between Scripture, tradition, and reason. Anglicans have a broad theological spectrum, ranging from High Church (closer to Catholicism) to Low Church (more Protestant in practice).

4. Baptists

Founder: John Smyth (early 1600s)

Main Beliefs: Believer's baptism (adult baptism), congregational church governance, autonomy of the local church.

The Baptist movement originated in the early 17th century as part of the Radical Reformation. Baptists reject infant baptism, insisting that baptism is only for believers who can make a conscious profession of faith.

Baptists also practice congregational governance, meaning each local church is independent and self-governing. They are one of the largest Protestant groups in the world, especially in the United States, where groups like the Southern Baptist Convention are highly influential.

5. Methodism

Founder: John Wesley (1703–1791)

Main Beliefs: Arminian theology (free will in salvation), personal holiness, social justice.

Key Texts: The Book of Discipline.

Methodism arose in the 18th century as a revival movement within the Church of England. It was led by John Wesley, who emphasized personal holiness, evangelism, and social reform.

Unlike Calvinists, Methodists reject predestination, believing instead in free will and God's grace available to all. The Methodist Church became highly missionary-focused, spreading to America, Africa, and Asia.

Today, major Methodist groups include the United Methodist Church and the African Methodist Episcopal Church (AME).

Conclusion: The Diversity of Protestantism

Protestantism is immensely diverse, with each branch shaping the Christian faith in unique ways. Some emphasize highly structured liturgies, while others embrace free worship styles. Some uphold predestination, while others stress free will. Despite these differences, all Protestants are united by their commitment to Scripture, salvation through Christ, and a rejection of papal authority.

From the Lutherans in Germany to the Baptists in America, from the Anglicans in England to the Pentecostals in Africa, Protestantism remains a dynamic force in global Christianity, continually evolving while holding firm to its foundational principles.

Pentecostalism and Charismatic Christianity

Beliefs, worship style, and global influence.

Christianity has taken on many forms and expressions over the centuries, shaped by theological debates, cultural shifts, and historical events. Among these diverse movements, Pentecostalism and Charismatic Christianity stand out as one of the most influential and fastest-growing expressions of Christianity in the modern world. Defined by a strong emphasis on the Holy Spirit, spiritual gifts, and dynamic worship, Pentecostalism has transformed Christian worship, theology, and missionary work. Its offshoot, the Charismatic movement, has extended Pentecostal-style spirituality into mainline denominations, impacting millions of believers worldwide.

This section explores the origins, core beliefs, worship style, and global influence of Pentecostalism and Charismatic Christianity, highlighting how these movements have reshaped contemporary Christian faith and practice.

Origins of Pentecostalism

Pentecostalism traces its roots to the early 20th century, but its theological foundation reaches back to the New Testament Church. The movement is named after Pentecost, the biblical event in Acts 2 when the Holy Spirit descended upon the apostles, enabling them to speak in tongues and perform miracles. Pentecostals believe that this experience of Spirit baptism and supernatural gifts is not confined to the early Church but is available to all believers today.

The modern Pentecostal movement emerged during the Azusa Street Revival (1906–1909) in Los Angeles, led by William J. Seymour, an African American Holiness preacher. This revival, characterized by ecstatic worship, speaking in tongues, healings, and interracial gatherings, sparked a global movement that gave birth to major Pentecostal denominations such as:

The Assemblies of God (1914)
The Church of God in Christ (COGIC)
The Foursquare Church
The Pentecostal Holiness Church

Since its inception, Pentecostalism has spread rapidly across North America, Latin America, Africa, and Asia, profoundly shaping the landscape of modern Christianity.

Core Beliefs of Pentecostalism

Pentecostalism shares many beliefs with mainstream Protestant Christianity, including faith in Jesus Christ as Lord and Savior, the authority of Scripture, and the importance of evangelism. However, Pentecostals emphasize distinctive theological doctrines that set them apart from other Christian traditions.

1. Baptism in the Holy Spirit

Unlike many Christian denominations that view the reception of the Holy Spirit as occurring at conversion, Pentecostals believe in a distinct, post-conversion experience called Spirit baptism. This is an empowerment of believers for spiritual growth, bold evangelism, and supernatural gifts.

2. Speaking in Tongues (Glossolalia)

A key marker of Spirit baptism is speaking in tongues, which Pentecostals see as a sign that a believer has received the Holy Spirit. They differentiate between:

Personal prayer tongues (a private prayer language between the believer and God).

Public tongues (which require interpretation in a congregational setting).

3. Spiritual Gifts (Charismata)

Pentecostals embrace the continuation of spiritual gifts (1

Corinthians 12:8-10), including:
Healing (miraculous physical restoration).
Prophecy (divine messages for individuals or churches).
Words of knowledge and wisdom (supernatural insight).

4. Divine Healing and Miracles

Healing is a major focus in Pentecostal theology. Many Pentecostal churches hold healing services where believers pray for the sick, expecting miraculous recoveries. They often cite James 5:14-15, where the elders of the church anoint the sick and pray for healing.

5. Premillennial Eschatology

Most Pentecostals believe in the imminent return of Christ and hold to a premillennial eschatology, meaning they expect Christ to return before a literal 1,000-year reign on earth. Many also emphasize the role of modern Israel in end-times prophecy.

Pentecostal Worship Style

Worship in Pentecostal churches is highly expressive, spontaneous, and emotionally charged. While styles vary by culture, certain elements are universal:

Energetic Music and Praise – Pentecostal services feature lively worship music, often accompanied by drums, guitars, and keyboards. Congregants actively participate by clapping, lifting hands, dancing, and singing in tongues.

Prophetic Preaching – Sermons emphasize personal transformation, miracles, and empowerment by the Holy Spirit. Pastors often engage the audience with passionate and spontaneous preaching.

Extended Prayer and Altar Calls – Services frequently include altar calls where individuals seek prayer, healing, or Spirit baptism.

Manifestations of the Holy Spirit – It is common to see believers falling under the power of the Spirit, speaking in tongues, or expressing deep emotional responses.

The Charismatic Movement

While Pentecostalism developed as a distinct movement, similar practices and beliefs began appearing in mainline Protestant and Catholic churches in the 1960s and 1970s. This became known as the Charismatic movement.

Unlike Pentecostals, Charismatics remain within their original denominations (Catholic, Anglican, Methodist, etc.) but embrace spiritual gifts such as speaking in tongues, healing, and prophecy.

The Catholic Charismatic Renewal, for instance, has millions of adherents worldwide.

Many Charismatic churches are non-denominational and led by independent pastors and evangelists.

Charismatic Christianity has influenced global worship trends, particularly through contemporary Christian music (CCM) and large-scale revival meetings.

Pentecostalism's Global Influence

Pentecostalism is one of the fastest-growing movements in Christianity, with an estimated 600 million adherents worldwide. Its influence is especially strong in:

Latin America – Many former Catholics have embraced Pentecostalism, leading to a religious shift in countries like Brazil, Argentina, and Guatemala.

Africa – Indigenous Pentecostal churches thrive, often blending Christianity with African spiritual traditions.

Asia – Pentecostalism has exploded in countries like South Korea, India, and China, where underground churches emphasize miracles and healing.

The United States – Megachurches like Lakewood Church (Joel Osteen) and Bethel Church showcase Charismatic influence in mainstream Christianity.

Additionally, Pentecostalism has revolutionized Christian missions, using faith healing and miracle testimonies to evangelize in remote and resistant areas.

Criticisms and Controversies

Despite its widespread appeal, Pentecostalism has faced criticism from both secular and Christian circles:

Theological Concerns – Some Protestants argue that Pentecostals focus too much on spiritual experiences and miracles rather than doctrinal depth.

Prosperity Gospel – Certain Pentecostal preachers promote the "prosperity gospel," teaching that faith leads to financial success and physical health.

Excesses in Worship – Critics claim that some Pentecostal churches encourage emotionalism over sound theology, with extreme practices such as "holy laughter" or "being slain in the Spirit."

Despite these criticisms, Pentecostalism continues to thrive due to its passionate faith, emphasis on the supernatural, and adaptability to diverse cultures.

Conclusion

Pentecostalism and Charismatic Christianity have reshaped the global Christian landscape, bringing renewed emphasis on the Holy Spirit, spiritual gifts, and passionate worship. Their influence is seen in modern worship music, global missions, and new church movements.

As Pentecostalism continues to grow, it raises questions about the future of Christianity:

Will Pentecostalism merge with other traditions or remain distinct?

How will miracles and healings be understood in modern society?

Can Pentecostal churches balance emotional spirituality with deep theological reflection?

Regardless of the answers, Pentecostalism remains a defining force in the 21st-century Church, proving that the fire of Pentecost is still burning worldwide.

✝ Non-Trinitarian Christian Movements

Jehovah's Witnesses, Mormons, and other groups.

Christianity has traditionally been defined by its adherence to Trinitarian doctrine, the belief that God exists as three distinct persons—Father, Son, and Holy Spirit—yet is one being. This doctrine, formalized in the early ecumenical councils, has been the cornerstone of mainstream Christianity, shaping Catholicism, Eastern Orthodoxy, and most branches of Protestantism.

However, throughout history, various movements and sects have rejected the doctrine of the Trinity, advocating alternative theological interpretations of God, Jesus Christ, and the Holy Spirit. These movements, often labeled Non-Trinitarian Christian groups, maintain Christian identities yet diverge significantly from traditional Christianity in doctrine and practice.

Among the most well-known of these are Jehovah's Witnesses, The Church of Jesus Christ of Latter-day Saints (Mormons), Christadelphians, and Unitarian movements. These groups challenge the mainstream understanding of God's nature, the divinity of Christ, and salvation, making them subjects of both theological debate and historical controversy.

This section explores the origins, beliefs, and key distinctions of the major Non-Trinitarian Christian movements, examining how they have developed alongside and in contrast to mainstream Christianity.

Jehovah's Witnesses

Origins and History

Jehovah's Witnesses emerged in the late 19th century through the teachings of Charles Taze Russell (1852–1916), an American Bible student who rejected key doctrines of mainstream Christianity, particularly the Trinity, the immortality of the soul, and eternal hellfire.

Russell founded the Watch Tower Bible and Tract Society in 1881, publishing biblical interpretations that diverged from traditional Christianity. After his death, Joseph Franklin Rutherford took leadership, restructuring the movement into what became known as Jehovah's Witnesses in 1931.

Core Beliefs

Jehovah's Witnesses adhere to a strictly monotheistic belief system, rejecting the Trinity as unbiblical. Key doctrinal positions include:

God (Jehovah) is one, and Jesus is a created being – They believe that Jehovah alone is Almighty God, and that Jesus Christ is his first creation, a divine being but not equal to God.

Jesus is not God but the Archangel Michael – They teach that Jesus existed as the Archangel Michael before being born as a man and later exalted back to an angelic status after his resurrection.

The Holy Spirit is not a person – Unlike Trinitarians who believe in the personhood of the Holy Spirit, Jehovah's Witnesses view the Holy Spirit as God's active force, much like an impersonal energy.

Rejection of the cross – They believe that Jesus did not die on a cross but on a "torture stake", as they claim the cross was a later pagan addition to Christianity.

No belief in Hell – Jehovah's Witnesses reject the concept of eternal punishment, teaching that the wicked are simply annihilated.

Strict neutrality and evangelism – They refuse military service, political involvement, and national allegiance, emphasizing door-to-door evangelism as central to their faith.

Distinctive Practices

Use of the New World Translation of the Bible, which reflects their theological positions.

No celebrations of Christmas, Easter, or birthdays, as they associate these with pagan origins.

Disfellowshipping, or excommunication, for members who violate doctrinal teachings.

The Church of Jesus Christ of Latter-day Saints (Mormons)

Origins and History

The Latter-day Saint (LDS) movement, commonly known as Mormonism, was founded by Joseph Smith in 1830 after he claimed to receive divine revelations and golden plates from an angel named Moroni. These revelations were published as The Book of Mormon, which Mormons regard as scripture alongside the Bible.

The movement grew rapidly but faced severe persecution, leading Mormons to migrate westward under Brigham Young, eventually settling in Utah. Today, the LDS Church is one of the largest and fastest-growing religious groups, with over 16 million members worldwide.

Core Beliefs

Mormon theology diverges radically from traditional Christianity, particularly regarding the nature of God, Jesus Christ, and human destiny.

God was once a man – Mormons believe that God (Heavenly Father) was once a mortal man who achieved godhood, suggesting that humans too can become gods.

Jesus is the literal son of God – Unlike traditional Christianity, Mormons believe Jesus is the literal offspring of God the Father and a Heavenly Mother.

The Trinity is three distinct beings – Rather than a single God in three persons, Mormons teach that the Father, Son, and Holy Spirit are separate gods, forming a Godhead rather than a Trinity.

Exaltation and Eternal Progression – Humans are seen as potential gods in the making who, through obedience and temple ordinances, can become divine beings ruling their own planets.

Additional Scriptures – In addition to the Bible, Mormons consider The Book of Mormon, The Doctrine and Covenants, and The Pearl of Great Price as divinely inspired scripture.

Distinctive Practices

Temple rituals, including baptisms for the dead and celestial marriage.

Missionary work, with young men expected to serve two-year missions worldwide.

Health code (Word of Wisdom), prohibiting alcohol, tobacco, coffee, and tea.

Other Non-Trinitarian Movements

Christadelphians

Founded in the 19th century by John Thomas, Christadelphians reject the Trinity and the immortality of the soul.

They believe Jesus is God's Son but not divine, and that the Holy Spirit is God's power, not a person.

Oneness Pentecostals

Unlike most Pentecostals, Oneness Pentecostals reject the Trinity, teaching instead that God is one person who manifests as Father, Son, and Holy Spirit at different times.

This belief is called Modalism, an ancient heresy condemned by the early Church.

Unitarianism

Unitarianism denies the divinity of Christ and sees him as a great moral teacher rather than God.

Many Unitarians are highly liberal and focus on ethics rather than supernatural beliefs.

Conclusion

Non-Trinitarian Christian movements challenge the central theological tenets of mainstream Christianity, particularly the nature of God, the divinity of Christ, and salvation. While these groups identify as Christian, their theological deviations have led mainline churches to view them as outside traditional Christianity.

Despite this, Jehovah's Witnesses, Mormons, and other Non-Trinitarian groups continue to grow, particularly through active missionary efforts and strong community structures.

Their rise raises important questions for Christian theology:

Is the Trinity essential for Christian identity?

Can alternative understandings of Jesus still be considered Christian?

How should mainstream Christianity engage with these groups?

Regardless of where one stands, Non-Trinitarian Christianity remains an influential force, shaping theological debates and expanding the diversity of Christian belief worldwide.

Christianity and Science

The relationship between faith and scientific discovery.

The relationship between Christianity and science has been one of complexity, tension, and cooperation throughout history. At various points, the Christian faith has both nurtured and challenged scientific discovery, influencing the way humans understand the natural world. From the medieval church's patronage of learning to the Galileo affair, and from Newton's theological reflections on the cosmos to modern debates over evolution and genetics, Christianity has never been wholly separate from scientific thought.

While secular narratives often portray faith and science as inherently opposed, this perspective overlooks centuries of intellectual exchange, where Christian scholars and scientists played foundational roles in advancing human knowledge. The scientific method, universities, and even modern physics owe much to the Christian intellectual tradition.

This section explores the historical relationship between Christianity and science, examining both harmony and conflict. It also considers modern areas of debate, such as evolution, cosmology, and bioethics, and reflects on how Christianity continues to engage with scientific discovery today.

Christianity's Role in the Development of Science

Far from being an obstacle to scientific progress, Christianity played a crucial role in its formation. In the Middle Ages, the Church established universities across Europe, where the study of natural philosophy (the precursor to science) was encouraged. Many of the greatest scientific pioneers were deeply religious men, believing that the universe reflected divine order and rationality.

Medieval and Renaissance Contributions

The Rise of Universities – The modern university system traces its roots to Christian institutions like the University of Paris, Oxford, and Bologna, where theology and natural philosophy were studied together.

The Preservation of Knowledge – During the so-called "Dark Ages", Christian monks preserved and copied scientific texts, ensuring that Greek and Roman knowledge survived to influence later European scholars.

The Idea of a Rational Universe – The belief that God created an orderly cosmos led Christian thinkers to develop early scientific principles, such as cause and effect, classification, and experimentation.

Christian Scientists and Their Legacy

Nicholas Copernicus (1473–1543) – A Catholic cleric who formulated the heliocentric model of the solar system, challenging the geocentric view held at the time.

Johannes Kepler (1571–1630) – A devout Christian who discovered the laws of planetary motion, believing that scientific discovery was a way to understand God's design.

Isaac Newton (1643–1727) – One of the most influential scientists in history, Newton saw physics as a means of uncovering God's divine laws of nature. He spent as much time writing theological works as scientific ones.

Such examples illustrate that science was never divorced from faith. In many ways, Christian theology provided the intellectual framework that made modern scientific investigation possible.

The Galileo Controversy: Faith vs. Science?

One of the most famous episodes in the perceived conflict between Christianity and science is the Galileo affair. In the early 17th century, Galileo Galilei (1564–1642) promoted heliocentrism, the idea that the Earth orbits the Sun. This was seen as contradicting certain biblical passages and the Aristotelian geocentric model, which was accepted by the Church at the time.

While secular accounts often depict Galileo as a martyr for science, the reality is more nuanced:

The Church Initially Supported Galileo – Early on, many Church officials were open to heliocentrism, but political and theological pressures complicated their stance.

The Conflict Was Partly Political – Galileo's public ridicule of the Pope in his writings contributed to his trial and house arrest.

The Church Later Accepted Heliocentrism – The Catholic Church eventually recognized the validity of Galileo's ideas, though it took centuries to fully acknowledge the error in his condemnation.

The Galileo affair remains a symbol of faith-science tensions, but it also shows that scientific progress was never wholly suppressed by Christianity.

Evolution and Creation: The Modern Divide

Perhaps the most significant modern controversy between Christianity and science revolves around evolution.

Darwin's Challenge

When Charles Darwin (1809–1882) published On the Origin of Species in 1859, it revolutionized the way humans understood life's development. Evolutionary theory suggested that species arose through natural selection, contradicting literal interpretations of Genesis, which described God creating the world in six days.

Christian Responses to Evolution

Young Earth Creationism – Some Christians reject evolution entirely, insisting on a literal reading of Genesis, where the Earth is only 6,000–10,000 years old.

Theistic Evolution – Others accept evolution but see it as guided by God, viewing Genesis as poetic rather than scientific.

Intelligent Design – A middle position that argues for scientific evidence of design in nature, rejecting pure Darwinism but not necessarily all forms of evolution.

While atheists often use evolution to challenge Christianity, many scientists—including devout Christians—embrace evolution while maintaining their faith.

Christianity and Cosmology: The Big Bang and Beyond

Christianity has also engaged deeply with cosmology, the study of the universe's origins.

The Big Bang Theory – Ironically, the Big Bang Theory was first proposed by a Catholic priest and physicist, Georges Lemaître (1894–1966). Many Christians saw it as compatible with Genesis, as it suggests the universe had a beginning.

Fine-Tuning and the Anthropic Principle – Modern physics has discovered that the universe appears finely tuned for life, leading some Christian thinkers to argue that this points to a Creator.

Rather than conflicting, scientific cosmology and Christian theology often complement each other, as both seek to understand the origins and purpose of existence.

Christianity and Bioethics: Moral Questions in Science

Science has raised new ethical challenges, particularly in areas like genetics, artificial intelligence, and medical advancements.

Key Bioethical Debates

Embryonic Stem Cell Research – Christian ethicists debate whether it is moral to use embryonic cells for medical research.

Artificial Intelligence and Human Dignity – Can AI possess consciousness? What does Christianity say about human uniqueness?

Cloning and Genetic Engineering – Should humans alter DNA, and what are the theological implications?

Christianity provides an ethical framework that many scientists turn to when considering the limits of technology.

Conclusion: Can Science and Christianity Coexist?

Despite past tensions, Christianity and science are not inherently at war. Many of the greatest scientists were devout Christians, and today, many Christian scientists contribute to fields like physics, biology, and medicine.

Key Takeaways:

Christianity helped develop the foundations of science by promoting rational inquiry.

Many scientists throughout history were Christian believers who saw science as a way to understand God's creation.

Conflicts, such as Galileo's trial and the evolution debate, are complex, often involving political and cultural factors, not just theology.

Science and Christianity continue to engage in ethical questions, particularly in bioethics, AI, and cosmology.

In the end, the question is not whether Christianity and science can coexist, but how they can continue to inform and challenge each other, enriching human understanding of both the physical world and the divine.

Christianity and Politics

The influence of Christianity on government and society.

From the moment Christianity emerged in the ancient Roman world, its relationship with politics has been both dynamic and transformative. At its core, Christianity was never merely a private or personal faith—it carried profound implications for how societies should be structured, how rulers should govern, and how justice, law, and morality should be defined. Whether as a persecuted minority in the Roman Empire, a dominant force in medieval Europe, or a voice in modern democratic debates, Christianity has played an essential role in shaping government and society.

Yet, this relationship has been complex. At times, Christianity has been a force of political stability and moral guidance; at others, it has been the source of conflict, division, and even oppression. It has inspired movements for freedom and human rights, yet also been used to justify authoritarian rule. This chapter explores the historical role of Christianity in politics, its influence on government structures, its involvement in key social movements, and its continuing presence in contemporary political discourse.

Christianity's Role in Early Political Thought
The New Testament and the Roman Empire

The earliest Christians lived under the rule of the Roman Empire, a vast political structure that often viewed them with suspicion. The New Testament reflects a nuanced approach to political authority.

Jesus himself said, "Render unto Caesar what is Caesar's, and to God what is God's" (Matthew 22:21)—a phrase that has been interpreted to mean both submission to government and the recognition of divine authority above it.

Paul's letter to the Romans urges believers to respect governing authorities, stating that "there is no authority except that which God has established" (Romans 13:1-7).

Yet, while Christians were encouraged to obey civil laws, they also saw themselves as citizens of the Kingdom of God, a higher order that transcended earthly politics. This tension between earthly government and divine authority has shaped Christian political thought for centuries.

The Conversion of Constantine and Christian Rule

The biggest political shift for Christianity came in the 4th century, when Emperor Constantine converted to Christianity and issued the Edict of Milan (313 AD), legalizing the faith. No longer a persecuted minority, Christianity began to intertwine with political power:

The Byzantine Empire made Christianity the state religion under Emperor Theodosius I (380 AD), setting the stage for theocratic rule.

The idea of a "Christian empire" took root, where rulers were seen as divinely appointed.

Bishops and church leaders gained significant influence over political decisions, leading to centuries of church-state relations in Europe.

This alliance between Christianity and government would shape the medieval world profoundly, giving rise to both moral leadership and corruption in political institutions.

Medieval Christendom: Church and State in Power

During the Middle Ages, Christianity was inseparable from political life. The Catholic Church became one of the most powerful institutions in Europe, with popes often exerting influence over kings and emperors.

The Papal States were governed directly by the pope, making the Church a political entity.

The Holy Roman Empire was founded on the idea of a Christian monarchy, where kings were crowned by popes.

Laws and social structures were deeply shaped by Christian doctrine, influencing ideas of justice, marriage, property, and governance.

However, conflicts between church and state were frequent. The Investiture Controversy (11th-12th century) was one of the greatest struggles, where popes and kings fought over who had the right to appoint bishops.

The medieval period demonstrated both the power and dangers of mixing Christianity with politics. While it upheld moral law and social order, it also led to corruption, power struggles, and even religious wars.

Christianity and the Birth of Democracy

One of the most profound political legacies of Christianity is its influence on modern democratic values. While some monarchs ruled with the belief in divine right, Christianity also sowed the seeds of individual rights, equality, and justice.

The Protestant Reformation and Political Change

The Protestant Reformation (16th century) was not just a religious movement—it had major political consequences:

Luther and Calvin argued that individuals should have direct access to God, which weakened the authority of centralized rulers and empowered local governance.

The Reformation led to the idea of separating church and state, especially in places like the Netherlands and England.

Religious pluralism forced societies to develop systems of tolerance and democratic rule to accommodate different beliefs.

Christianity and Human Rights

Many foundational ideas in modern human rights and democracy have Christian roots:

The belief in the sanctity of life and human dignity led to opposition to slavery and injustice.

Christian groups, such as the Quakers, were early pioneers in abolitionist movements.

The concept of "all men being created equal", found in the U.S. Declaration of Independence, is deeply influenced by Christian moral philosophy.

From the Magna Carta (1215) to the U.S. Constitution, Christian thought has helped shape ideas of justice, governance, and freedom.

Christianity in Modern Political Debates
The Rise of Secularism

In the modern era, Christianity has had to navigate increasing secularism. Many governments have adopted separation of church and state, ensuring religion does not dictate political decisions.

Yet, Christianity remains a strong political force, influencing debates on:

Abortion and bioethics

Marriage and family structures

Religious freedom and minority rights

Social justice and welfare policies

Christian groups advocate on both sides of political issues. Some fight for conservative moral values, while others push for progressive social justice initiatives.

Christian Political Movements Today

The Christian Right (U.S. and beyond) – Advocates for traditional family values, pro-life policies, and religious freedom.

Christian Social Justice Movements – Focus on helping the poor, racial reconciliation, and refugees (e.g., Catholic Social Teaching, the World Council of Churches).

Liberation Theology – A movement in Latin America that combines Christianity with Marxist thought to advocate for the oppressed.

Despite changes in society, Christianity continues to shape laws, culture, and moral debates worldwide.

Conclusion: Christianity's Political Legacy and Future

The relationship between Christianity and politics is not a simple one. Christianity has built kingdoms and torn them down, inspired liberation movements and authoritarian regimes, and shaped the moral consciousness of nations.

Today, the role of Christianity in politics remains a subject of debate. Some argue that faith should stay out of government, while others believe Christian morality must guide national policies.

Yet, regardless of one's stance, history shows that Christianity has been one of the most powerful forces in shaping political life—a force that will likely continue influencing the world for generations to come.

Christianity and Other Religions

How Christianity relates to Judaism, Islam, Hinduism, Buddhism, etc.

Christianity is one of the world's most influential religions, shaping civilizations, moral frameworks, and cultures for over two thousand years. But Christianity does not exist in isolation—it emerged from Judaism, interacted with Islam, encountered Eastern traditions such as Hinduism and Buddhism, and engaged with indigenous and philosophical belief systems across the world. These relationships have ranged from deep theological dialogue to historical conflict, from mutual enrichment to efforts at conversion.

Understanding how Christianity relates to other religions provides insight into its identity, its points of intersection with other faiths, and the theological debates that continue to shape interreligious dialogue today.

Christianity and Judaism: A Family Relationship

Of all world religions, Christianity shares the deepest historical and theological connection with Judaism. Jesus himself was Jewish, as were his earliest disciples. The Old Testament, the Hebrew Bible, forms the foundation of Christian Scripture. Christianity can be seen as an offshoot of Judaism that later developed into its own distinct tradition.

Similarities

Monotheism – Both Judaism and Christianity believe in one God, the Creator of the universe.

Sacred Texts – Christianity's Old Testament is largely identical to the Hebrew Scriptures.

Moral Law – Both religions share ethical teachings, particularly those found in the Ten Commandments.

Messianic Hope – While Jews still anticipate the coming of the Messiah, Christians believe Jesus was that Messiah.

Key Differences

Jesus Christ – Judaism does not recognize Jesus as the Messiah or the Son of God.

The New Covenant – Christianity teaches that Jesus established a New Covenant, replacing the old Mosaic Law, whereas Judaism continues to uphold the Torah.

The Role of Works vs. Grace – Judaism traditionally emphasizes adherence to law and practice, whereas Christianity teaches that salvation comes through grace by faith in Jesus.

Historical Relationship

The history between Christianity and Judaism has been tragic and complex. Early Christians distanced themselves from Judaism, especially after the destruction of the Jewish Temple in 70 AD. Over time, Christianity became dominant in Europe, often leading to anti-Jewish sentiment and persecution, including medieval expulsions and accusations of deicide (the killing of God).

In the modern era, especially after the Holocaust, Christian-Jewish relations have improved significantly, with many Christian denominations repudiating anti-Semitic teachings and fostering dialogue.

Christianity and Islam: Two Monotheistic Giants

Islam and Christianity are the two largest religions in the world today, both tracing their roots to Abraham and sharing a belief in one, omnipotent God. Islam emerged in the 7th century with the teachings of Muhammad, who Muslims believe to be the final prophet.

Similarities

Monotheism – Both believe in one God who is sovereign over creation.

Reverence for Jesus – Islam acknowledges Jesus (Isa) as a prophet, though not divine.

Moral Teachings – Both faiths emphasize prayer, charity, and judgment after death.

Key Differences

The Nature of God – Christianity teaches that God is Trinitarian (Father, Son, and Holy Spirit), while Islam insists on absolute oneness (Tawhid).

The Status of Jesus – In Christianity, Jesus is the Son of God and Savior. In Islam, he is a prophet, not divine, and was not crucified.

The Role of Scripture – Christians view the Bible as God's final revelation, whereas Muslims believe the Qur'an is the ultimate and unchanged Word of God.

Historical Relationship

The historical relationship between Christianity and Islam has been both cooperative and conflict-ridden.

The Crusades (11th-13th centuries) were a major point of conflict, as Christian and Muslim forces fought over control of the Holy Land.

In modern times, interfaith dialogue has improved, but missionary efforts and political conflicts continue to be sources of tension.

Despite differences, Christian-Muslim dialogue remains an important global effort in addressing issues of peace, justice, and religious tolerance.

Christianity and Hinduism: The Encounter of East and West

Hinduism, the oldest major world religion, differs greatly from Christianity in both belief and practice. Whereas Christianity is monotheistic with a linear view of history, Hinduism is polytheistic (though some sects are monistic) and cyclical in its understanding of time.

Similarities

Ethical Teachings – Both emphasize compassion, selflessness, and devotion.

The Concept of a Divine Incarnation – Hinduism's avatars (such as Krishna) bear similarities to the idea of Christ's incarnation.

Key Differences

God's Nature – Hinduism sees God as manifesting in multiple forms, while Christianity believes in one God with three persons.

Salvation – Christianity teaches salvation through Jesus, while Hinduism offers multiple paths to enlightenment (karma, devotion, meditation).

The Afterlife – Christianity teaches heaven and hell, whereas Hinduism believes in reincarnation.

Historical Relationship

Christianity arrived in India in the 1st century AD, possibly with the apostle Thomas. Christian missions in the colonial era led to both conversions and conflicts, but today there is interfaith dialogue between Hindus and Christians, especially in discussions on spirituality and ethics.

Christianity and Buddhism: The Path of Wisdom and Salvation

Buddhism, like Hinduism, originated in India but rejects the notion of a personal God. Instead, it focuses on the end of suffering through enlightenment.

Similarities

Moral Living – Both stress compassion, peace, and overcoming selfish desires.

Transformation of the Soul – Christianity speaks of spiritual rebirth, while Buddhism speaks of awakening.

Key Differences

God – Christianity is theistic, while Buddhism is nontheistic.

Salvation – Christianity teaches salvation by grace through Jesus, whereas Buddhism teaches self-liberation through enlightenment.

The Soul – Buddhism denies a permanent self (anatman), whereas Christianity believes in an eternal soul.

Historical Relationship

Christian missionaries have engaged with Buddhism, but conversion efforts have been limited. Instead, Buddhism and Christianity have influenced each other in areas of mysticism, meditation, and ethics.

Christianity and Indigenous Religions

Christianity has had a complex relationship with indigenous spiritual traditions, often leading to conflict, suppression, and syncretism.

In the Americas, many indigenous beliefs were suppressed by European colonizers, but some merged with Christian practices (e.g., Day of the Dead in Mexico).

In Africa, Christianity adapted to local traditions, leading to African Independent Churches that blend Christianity with traditional spirituality.

In Asia and the Pacific, Christian missionaries translated the Bible into native languages, leading to the spread of Christianity but also cultural clashes.

Conclusion: Towards Interfaith Dialogue

Christianity's relationship with other religions has been marked by both tension and dialogue. While theological differences remain, modern interfaith efforts emphasize mutual understanding, respect, and cooperation.

Today, in an era of globalization, the question is not just how

Christianity relates to other religions, but how people of all faiths can coexist peacefully while remaining true to their beliefs.

Challenges and the Future of Christianity

Secularism, modernity, and the future of the faith.

Christianity, a faith that has shaped civilizations, inspired revolutions, and provided the foundation for countless moral and philosophical traditions, now stands at a crossroads. In the modern world, it faces challenges unlike any it has encountered in its two-thousand-year history. While external persecution has always been a reality, today's greatest struggles are often internal—questions of identity, adaptation, and survival in an increasingly secular and pluralistic world.

The decline of religious affiliation, the rise of scientific rationalism, the erosion of traditional moral frameworks, and the diversification of worldviews have all contributed to a transformation of Christianity's role in society. At the same time, Christianity continues to thrive in unexpected places, taking new forms, finding new expressions, and proving that it is, at its core, a resilient and dynamic faith.

This chapter explores the key challenges Christianity faces in the modern world and speculates on its possible futures.

The Rise of Secularism: A Post-Christian World?

Perhaps the most significant challenge Christianity faces today is the rise of secularism—a worldview that either rejects or ignores religious beliefs in favor of reason, science, and human autonomy. Across much of the Western world, especially in Europe and North America, Christian influence has been steadily declining.

The Decline of Religious Affiliation

Church attendance has plummeted in many Western nations. In

places like France, the UK, and Scandinavia, Christian identity is often cultural rather than spiritual.

Younger generations increasingly identify as "religiously unaffiliated" or "spiritual but not religious."

In some cases, Christianity is viewed as irrelevant, outdated, or even oppressive, particularly on issues of morality and social justice.

The Influence of Secular Humanism

Secularism promotes human reason, ethics, and naturalism over divine revelation.

Concepts like objective morality, sin, and divine judgment are increasingly dismissed as outdated or unnecessary.

Many secular movements champion progressive social causes, often putting them at odds with traditional Christian teachings on topics like gender, sexuality, and family.

Christian Responses to Secularism

Some Christian groups have embraced modernity, adapting their theology to fit contemporary values.

Others have chosen to resist secular influence, emphasizing traditional doctrine and moral teachings.

Apologetics and philosophical engagement have seen a revival, as Christian scholars seek to reconcile faith with reason.

Secularism presents Christianity with a challenge and an opportunity—either retreat into obscurity or engage with the world in new, creative ways.

Science and Christianity: Conflict or Coexistence?

For centuries, Christianity and science have had a complicated relationship. While early Christian scholars laid the groundwork for scientific progress, the modern era has seen growing tension between religious belief and scientific discovery.

Challenges Posed by Science

Evolution vs. Creationism – The theory of evolution challenges literal interpretations of Genesis, leading to debates over whether the Bible should be read metaphorically or scientifically.

The Big Bang and Cosmology – While some see the Big Bang as evidence of a Creator, others use it to argue that God is unnecessary in explaining the origins of the universe.

Advancements in Neuroscience – The study of the brain has led some to question the existence of the soul, a core doctrine of Christian anthropology.

Christianity's Adaptation

Some theologians embrace scientific discoveries, seeing no conflict between faith and reason.

The Catholic Church and many Protestant groups now accept evolution as compatible with the belief in a divine Creator.

Science and faith need not be enemies—many of history's greatest scientists (Newton, Galileo, Pascal, and even Darwin) had deep religious convictions.

The future of Christianity will depend, in part, on how it navigates scientific progress without compromising its core spiritual truths.

Moral and Social Challenges

Shifting Moral Landscapes

Christianity has historically shaped Western morality, but today, many of its ethical teachings are being challenged.

Sexuality and Gender – Traditional Christian views on marriage, gender, and sexuality are often seen as intolerant or outdated.

The Role of Women – Some criticize Christianity for perpetuating patriarchal structures, while others highlight women's empowerment within the faith.

Religious Freedom vs. Progressive Values – Tension arises when Christian beliefs come into conflict with legal or social norms (e.g., same-sex marriage, abortion rights, religious expression in public spaces).

A Call for Renewal?

In response to these changes, many Christian communities have undergone reforms:

Some denominations have adapted their teachings to align with modern ethics.

Others have doubled down on traditional beliefs, emphasizing countercultural faithfulness.

The future of Christianity depends on how it engages with the moral debates of the modern world—will it adapt, resist, or find a middle ground?

The Future of Christianity: Three Possible Paths

What does the future hold for Christianity? While predicting the fate of a two-thousand-year-old faith is impossible, three potential paths emerge:

1. Christianity Becomes a Minority Faith in the West but Thrives Elsewhere

As secularization grows in Europe and North America, Christianity may decline in the West.

However, Christianity is growing rapidly in Africa, Latin America, and Asia.

The future church may be less Western and more global, shaped by cultures outside its European roots.

2. Christianity Adapts and Evolves

Some predict Christianity will modernize, adopting more flexible theological positions.

A focus on spirituality over doctrine may allow it to coexist with pluralism.

The Church may emphasize experience over dogma, encouraging mysticism, meditation, and interfaith dialogue.

3. Christianity Experiences a Revival

Historically, Christianity has flourished after periods of decline.

Some anticipate a new religious awakening, sparked by a renewed search for meaning in an increasingly materialistic world.

As people seek purpose beyond secularism, Christianity could experience a resurgence.

Conclusion: The Challenge of Faith in a Changing World

Christianity has survived persecutions, intellectual revolutions, and cultural upheavals. Yet, the modern world presents unique challenges that require adaptation, resilience, and a renewed vision.

Will Christianity fade into the background, a relic of the past? Or will it find new ways to engage with the world, keeping its ancient truths relevant for future generations?

The answer depends not only on theologians, scholars, and pastors but on individual believers—those willing to wrestle with faith, embrace mystery, and live out the teachings of Christ in an ever-changing world.

✝ Further Reading

For those who wish to delve deeper into the study of Christianity, its doctrines, history, theology, and influence, the following books provide a solid foundation. This list includes classic theological works, historical studies, and modern interpretations, ensuring readers have a well-rounded approach to understanding Christianity from various perspectives.

1. The Bible and Its Study

A deep understanding of Christianity begins with its sacred text. The following versions and study aids are indispensable:

The Holy Bible (Multiple Translations) – Recommended versions include:

King James Version (KJV) – A literary masterpiece with traditional phrasing.

New International Version (NIV) – A widely accessible and modern translation.

English Standard Version (ESV) – Balances readability and scholarly accuracy.

New Revised Standard Version (NRSV) – Used widely in academic and theological circles.

"How to Read the Bible for All Its Worth" – Gordon D. Fee & Douglas Stuart

A guide to understanding different biblical genres and how to interpret scripture effectively.

"The New Testament and the People of God" – N.T. Wright

A historical and theological analysis of the New Testament in its first-century context.

"Introduction to the Old Testament" – Tremper Longman III
A scholarly yet accessible introduction to the historical and literary background of the Old Testament.

2. Christian Theology and Doctrine

For those seeking a deeper theological grounding, these books provide a solid framework:

"Mere Christianity" – C.S. Lewis
A classic defense of Christian faith, presenting a rational case for belief.

"The Cost of Discipleship" – Dietrich Bonhoeffer
A powerful work on Christian ethics and the true meaning of following Christ.

"Systematic Theology" – Wayne Grudem
A comprehensive guide to Christian doctrines from an evangelical perspective.

"Theology for Beginners" – Frank Sheed
A clear introduction to Christian theology, written in an engaging style.

"The Knowledge of the Holy" – A.W. Tozer
A devotional study of the attributes of God.

"The Trinity" – Karl Rahner
An exploration of one of Christianity's core mysteries: the Father, Son, and Holy Spirit.

"Simply Christian" – N.T. Wright
A modern, accessible introduction to the heart of Christian belief.

3. Church History

Understanding Christianity's development over time is essential. The following books trace its origins, expansion, and influence:

"The History of Christianity" – Justo L. González
A readable yet scholarly history of Christianity from its beginnings

to the present.

"The Story of Christianity" (Volumes 1 & 2) – Justo L. González
A highly recommended two-volume series covering the early church through modern Christianity.

"Church History in Plain Language" – Bruce L. Shelley
A narrative-driven account of Christianity's historical development.

"The Early Church" – Henry Chadwick
A classic work covering the first few centuries of Christian history.

"The Reformation: A History" – Diarmaid MacCulloch
A definitive history of the Protestant Reformation and its consequences.

"Christianity: The First Three Thousand Years" – Diarmaid MacCulloch
A sweeping and in-depth history of Christianity, from its Jewish roots to the modern day.

4. Christian Apologetics

For those interested in defending the faith and engaging with skepticism, these books offer thoughtful arguments:

"The Case for Christ" – Lee Strobel
A journalist's investigation into the historical evidence for Jesus.

"Reasonable Faith" – William Lane Craig
A philosophical and theological defense of Christian belief.

"The Problem of Pain" – C.S. Lewis
A discussion on why suffering exists in a world created by a good God.

"Tactics: A Game Plan for Discussing Your Christian Convictions" – Gregory Koukl
A practical guide for engaging in thoughtful discussions about Christianity.

5. Christian Philosophy and Ethics

For those who want to explore Christianity's moral teachings and impact on society, these books provide insightful discussions:

"Confessions" – Saint Augustine

One of the greatest spiritual autobiographies ever written, reflecting on sin, grace, and redemption.

"The Abolition of Man" – C.S. Lewis

A defense of moral absolutes and the dangers of moral relativism.

"Christian Ethics: An Introduction" – J. Philip Wogaman

A survey of Christian moral thought across history.

"Kingdom Ethics" – David P. Gushee & Glen H. Stassen

A discussion of Jesus' ethical teachings and their modern application.

6. Denominational Studies

For those interested in the various branches of Christianity, these books offer insight into different traditions:

"Roman Catholicism: A History" – Thomas Bokenkotter

A comprehensive introduction to Catholic beliefs, structure, and history.

"The Orthodox Church" – Timothy Ware

A detailed guide to Eastern Orthodoxy's theology, traditions, and history.

"Christianity's Dangerous Idea: The Protestant Revolution" – Alister McGrath

A history of Protestantism and its ongoing impact on Christianity.

"Pentecostalism: The World Their Parish" – David Martin

An analysis of the fastest-growing movement within Christianity.

7. Christianity and Culture

Christianity has influenced art, literature, politics, and science. These books examine its broader cultural significance:

"Jesus Through the Centuries" – Jaroslav Pelikan

A study of how different ages and cultures have understood Jesus.

"The Rise of Christianity" - Rodney Stark

An exploration of how Christianity spread and thrived in the Roman Empire.

"Dominion: How the Christian Revolution Remade the World" - Tom Holland

A powerful examination of Christianity's enduring influence on Western civilization.

"The Scandal of the Evangelical Mind" - Mark A. Noll

A critique of anti-intellectualism in modern Christianity.

8. Christianity and Science

For readers interested in the relationship between faith and scientific discovery, these books explore the dialogue between Christianity and science:

"The Language of God" - Francis Collins

A perspective from a geneticist and Christian on the compatibility of science and faith.

"Science and Religion: A New Introduction" - Alister McGrath

A balanced discussion of historical and modern interactions between Christianity and science.

"The Reason for God" - Timothy Keller

A defense of Christianity addressing scientific and philosophical objections.

Christianity and Other Religions

"The Sacred and the Profane: The Nature of Religion" - Mircea Eliade

Explores the distinction between sacred and profane time and space, a crucial concept for understanding religious experience, including Christianity.

"Patterns in Comparative Religion" - Mircea Eliade

A study of religious symbols, myths, and archetypes across various faiths, with themes relevant to Christian theology and ritual.

Christianity and Culture

"The Myth of the Eternal Return" – Mircea Eliade

Examines the idea of cyclical and linear time in religious traditions, which contrasts with Christianity's unique historical and eschatological perspective.

"A History of Religious Ideas" (Volumes 1-3) – Mircea Eliade

A monumental survey of religious ideas from prehistoric times to modernity, including the evolution of Christian thought.

Epilogue
Christianity in an Age of Change

As we reach the conclusion of this exploration into Christianity, we find ourselves at a crossroads. Christianity is not merely a historical phenomenon or an abstract theological system; it is a living, evolving faith that continues to shape and be shaped by the world around it. It has endured for over two millennia, adapting to shifting cultural landscapes, surviving persecution, inspiring revolutions, and influencing the moral and intellectual foundations of societies across the globe. But what does the future hold for Christianity? And more importantly, what role does it play in the lives of individuals today?

To understand where Christianity is going, we must remember where it began. A movement that started with a small group of disciples in first-century Palestine has grown into the largest and most widespread religion on Earth. From the catacombs of Rome to the towering cathedrals of Europe, from underground churches in persecuted nations to the digital ministries of the modern era, Christianity has found ways to persist, to transform, and to thrive. It has split into denominations, engaged in fierce theological debates, and wrestled with the challenges of modernity. And yet, at its core, Christianity has remained anchored in the figure of Jesus Christ—a man whose life and teachings continue to inspire billions.

But Christianity does not exist in isolation. It faces an age of radical change—an era defined by secularism, scientific advancements, political upheavals, and shifting social values. In many parts of the world, religious belief is declining, churches are closing, and faith traditions are being questioned. And yet, in other regions, Christianity is experiencing unprecedented growth, particularly in Africa, Asia, and Latin America. The faith is neither dying nor stagnant; it is simply evolving.

One of the great questions of our time is how Christianity will navigate the modern world. Can it maintain its relevance in societies that increasingly prioritize science, individualism, and secular ethics? Can it respond to contemporary moral dilemmas with wisdom and compassion? Can it unite rather than divide, inspire rather than condemn, and renew its vision for a world in need of meaning?

If history is any indication, Christianity has the remarkable ability to reinvent itself while remaining true to its fundamental message. The faith that survived the fall of Rome, the upheaval of the Reformation, the Age of Enlightenment, and the rise of modern technology is not likely to disappear anytime soon. It will continue to be challenged, but it will also continue to offer hope. Whether in the form of traditional liturgies or new expressions of faith in digital spaces, whether through intellectual engagement with science or passionate calls for social justice, Christianity will remain a force that cannot be ignored.

Yet beyond its historical, theological, and institutional dimensions, Christianity remains, at its heart, a deeply personal journey. For millions, it is not merely an idea, a tradition, or a cultural force—it is the foundation of their lives, the source of their identity, and the lens through which they make sense of existence. It offers the promise of redemption, the call to love, and the challenge to seek truth.

So, as we close this book, we leave with an open question: What will Christianity mean to you? Will it be an academic study, a historical curiosity, a subject for debate? Or will it be something more—an invitation to explore, to question, to engage with a tradition that has shaped the course of human history and continues to offer a vision of faith, hope, and love?

Whatever your answer, Christianity remains one of the most profound and enduring forces in the world. It is a story still being written, and perhaps, in some way, you are part of that story too.

THE END

Join The SUMIT Community

The journey of understanding doesn't end with a single book—it's a lifelong pursuit. **SUMIT** was designed to bring clarity to the vast worlds of business, psychology, philosophy, history, religion, and beyond. Each book distills the essence of profound ideas, influential figures, and transformative concepts, making them accessible and actionable for learners like you.

But why stop at one book? **Join the SUMIT Community** and become part of a vibrant network of curious minds dedicated to exploring and mastering the greatest ideas across disciplines.

Dive Deeper into your favorite subjects
Stay Inspired with insights from a growing library of expertly summarized knowledge
Connect with a community of learners who value growth and understanding as much as you do

Scan the QR Code Below to Join Us Today!
Together, we can continue to explore, learn, and create a legacy of knowledge that shapes our lives and the world around us. Don't just read about ideas—live them with the SUMIT Community.
(It's free, and you can unsubscribe anytime.)

Religion Summit Collection

Embark on an enlightening journey across the beliefs that shape our world. The Religion Summit Collection is more than just a series of books – it's a personal voyage of discovery through the wisdom of ages. Each volume invites you to a "summit" of ideas where Eastern philosophies meet Western traditions, ancient teachings encounter modern questions, and curiosity sparks personal growth at every turn.

Join the countless readers who view the Religion Summit Collection as a must-have resource for expanding their horizons. If you long to connect the dots between faiths or seek wisdom to navigate your own life challenges, this series is your companion. Open your mind and heart to a summit of spiritual knowledge – and prepare to see the world's religions in a whole new light.

101 Religion Ideas - Explore Diverse Traditions, Deepen Your Perspective, and Enrich Your Spiritual Life

What if one book could open your mind to 101 profound insights from the world's great religions? 101 Religion Ideas is your gateway to understanding how centuries-old wisdom can empower and inspire your modern life. Unlock the wisdom of the world's religions – dive into 101 Religion Ideas today and embark on a transformative spiritual adventure.

CHRISTIANITY Summarized
A Complete Guide to the History, Beliefs, and Practices of the Christian Faith

For over two thousand years, Christianity has shaped civilizations, inspired revolutions, and transformed countless lives. But what is Christianity at its core? What do its followers truly believe? How did it evolve from a small group of disciples to the largest faith in the world?

ISLAM Summarized
A Concise Guide to Islamic Beliefs, History, Law, and Spirituality – Understanding Islam, the Qur'an, Shariah, Sufism, and Muslim Traditions

For over 1,400 years, Islam has shaped civilizations, inspired profound spiritual traditions, and influenced the course of world history. Yet, for many, it remains misunderstood—overshadowed by stereotypes and misconceptions.

BUDDHISM Summarized
A Complete Guide to Buddhist Philosophy, Teachings, and Meditation—From Theravāda to Zen and Tibetan Buddhism

For over 2,500 years, Buddhism has transformed the lives of millions, offering a path to inner peace, clarity, and awakening. But with its vast traditions, complex philosophies, and deep meditative practices, where does one begin? Are you ready to begin your journey?

HINDUISM Summarized
A Complete Guide to Hindu Philosophy, Scriptures, Gods, Rituals, and Spiritual Wisdom

Step into the vast, awe-inspiring world of Hinduism—a tradition that has shaped the spiritual consciousness of billions for over 5,000 years. This book is your gateway to understanding the profound wisdom, sacred rituals, divine deities, and timeless philosophies that define this extraordinary faith.

JUDAISM Summarized
Everything You Need to Know About Jewish Faith, Culture, and Tradition in One Essential Book

What does it truly mean to be Jewish? How has Judaism survived and thrived through centuries of exile, persecution, and renewal? Why do Jewish traditions, laws, and beliefs continue to shape the modern world? Understand Judaism. Appreciate its beauty. Engage with its future. Are you ready to discover the soul of a people?

NEW AGE & ESOTERICISM Summarized
A Complete Guide to Mysticism, Spiritual Awakening, Hidden Knowledge & Ancient Wisdom for Modern Seekers

Are you ready to uncover the secrets of the cosmos, awaken your inner power, and transform your spiritual destiny? New Age & Esotericism Summarized is your ultimate guide to the mystical realms of hidden knowledge, ancient wisdom, and modern spiritual evolution.

TAOISM Summarized
Taoist Philosophy, Spirituality, and Practice for Inner Peace, Balance, and Enlightenment

For centuries, Taoism has remained an enigmatic and profound philosophy, whispering its wisdom through the Dao De Jing, the paradoxes of Zhuangzi, and the graceful movements of Tai Chi. But what if you could grasp its essence in one compelling, immersive volume? Walk the path. Embrace the flow. Live in harmony with the Tao.

COMPARATIVE RELIGION Summarized
World Religions, Beliefs, and Spiritual Traditions – Exploring Sacred Texts, Practices, and Theories Across Faiths

Religion shapes civilizations, ignites wars, heals wounds, and inspires revolutions. It weaves itself into the fabric of our existence, influencing how we love, how we fear, and how we understand the unknown. But what happens when we step back and examine it all—side by side? This is the book you've been waiting for.

MYTH & FOLK RELIGIONS Summarized
Exploring Legends, Myths, and Sacred Traditions Across Cultures – From Creation Myths to Shamanism, Folklore, and Urban Legends

Myths are more than ancient tales—they are the pulse of civilizations, the echoes of forgotten gods, and the whispers of ancestors shaping our world. From the trickster gods who defy order to the heroic figures who battle darkness, myths illuminate the human experience in ways both mystical and profound.

WICCA & PAGANISM Summarized
Exploring Witchcraft, Magic, Rituals, Spells, Wiccan Beliefs, and Ancient Pagan Traditions

Unlock the Mysteries of Wicca and Paganism—A Journey into Ancient Wisdom, Magic, and Spiritual Awakening! No fluff. No gimmicks. Just raw, essential knowledge—distilled into an engaging, accessible volume that will deepen your understanding of Wicca, Witchcraft, and Pagan traditions.

Philosophy Summit Collection

Are you ready to explore the essence of wisdom and discover how great thinkers have shaped our world across centuries?

The Philosophy Summit Collection is your passport to a universe of philosophical ideas, bridging ancient and modern perspectives in a compelling, accessible way. Whether you're new to philosophy or seeking fresh insights, each volume in this groundbreaking series unpacks history's most influential schools of thought—revealing just how powerful these concepts can be for your everyday life.

Embark on your journey today, starting with our flagship title or any of the specialized volumes that catch your eye. It's time to climb the summit of thought and discover the heights of insight!

101 Philosophy Ideas - Timeless Wisdom to Empower Your Thinking and Your Life

Step into a fascinating introduction to philosophy that unites ancient wisdom with modern thought, giving you the ultimate roadmap to understand the history of philosophy and harness it for personal transformation. 101 Philosophy Ideas is your philosophy guide to the theories, thinkers, and debates that have shaped Western and Eastern philosophy alike—from Aristotle and Confucius to Nietzsche and beyond.

STOICISM Summarized
Ancient Wisdom for Modern Resilience: Mastering Mindset, Discipline, and Virtue for a Fulfilled Life

What if the secret to a powerful, unshakable mind was discovered over two thousand years ago? What if the path to true freedom, resilience, and success didn't lie in chasing wealth or external validation, but in mastering your own thoughts and actions? Are you ready to become Stoic?

EASTERN PHILOSOPHY Summarized
Timeless Wisdom from Hinduism, Buddhism, Daoism, and Confucianism for Mindfulness, Ethics, and Enlightenment

Transform Your Mind, Your Life, and Your Understanding of Reality! Are you ready to embark on a journey of transformation and insight? The path begins here.

EXISTENTIALISM Summarized
A Concise Guide to Freedom, Meaning, and the Absurd in Philosophy, Life, and Society

What does it mean to truly exist? Are we free, or are we trapped by forces beyond our control? If life has no inherent meaning, how do we create our own? This is more than philosophy—it's a call to action. Will you choose to live authentically? The abyss is staring back. Are you ready to stare back at it?

CRITICAL THINKING Summarized
The Ultimate Guide for Mastering Logic, Thinking Smarter, Spotting Lies and Making Better Decisions

We live in an era of misinformation, logical fallacies, and relentless persuasion—an age where half-truths spread faster than facts, and biased reasoning can lead entire societies astray. Critical Thinking Summarized is your weapon against deception, manipulation, and flawed reasoning.

ETHICS Summarized
Understanding Right and Wrong: A Complete Overview of Ethical Theories and Moral Reasoning

What is right? What is wrong? And why does it matter? From the dawn of civilization to the rise of artificial intelligence, humanity has wrestled with moral dilemmas that define our existence. Are you ready to think deeply, argue boldly, and challenge everything you thought you knew about morality?

PHILOSOPHY OF MIND Summarized
Exploring Consciousness, Free Will, AI, and the Nature of Thought

What is consciousness? Can we trust our perceptions? Do we have free will, or are we just complex machines running on neural code? If you've ever questioned reality, if you've ever wondered what makes you you—this is the book you've been waiting for.

POLITICAL PHILOSOPHY Summarized
Key Thinkers, Theories, and Debates on Power, Justice, and Freedom—From Plato to Postmodernism

What is justice? Who should rule? Can power ever be legitimate? This is no dry academic textbook. It's a bold, accessible, and razor-sharp and everything you need to master political philosophy—without the fluff, jargon, or confusion.. Understand the past. Decipher the present. Shape the future.

PHILOSOPHY OF RELIGION Summarized
A Concise Guide to Faith, Reason, God, and the Big Questions of Existence – Arguments, Critiques, and Key Debates in Religious Philosophy

What is the nature of God? Can faith and reason truly coexist? Why do some find deep meaning in religion while others reject it outright? Is there a way to settle the debate once and for all?

ANCIENT GREEK PHILOSOPHY Summarized
A Complete Guide to the Thinkers, Ideas, and Legacy of Classical Philosophy—From Socrates to Aristotle and Beyond

What does it mean to live a good life? What is truth, and how do we find it? Can reason shape society, or is chaos inevitable? These are not just questions for scholars in ivory towers—they are the foundations of how we think, act, and live today. The wisdom of the ancients awaits.

NIETZSCHE Summarized
Understanding Nietzsche: A Clear Guide to His Most Powerful and Controversial Ideas

What if everything you believed about truth, morality, and human nature was an illusion? What if God were dead, and you were left to forge your own path in a world without absolute meaning? If you are ready to think dangerously, live courageously, and go beyond good and evil, then this book is for you.

Business Summit Collection

A powerhouse series of business books delivering expert insights on entrepreneurship, business strategy, startups, and professional development. Designed for ambitious professionals, entrepreneurs, and aspiring business owners, this collection distills wisdom from top business minds and real-world success stories. Each volume in the series offers actionable guidance, proven strategies, and inspiring case studies – from launching innovative startups to mastering leadership and growth tactics. Whether you're looking to ignite a new venture or elevate your current business, the Business Summit Collection provides the knowledge and tools to thrive in the 21st-century business landscape. Join thousands of readers in discovering cutting-edge ideas and practical advice to drive your success.

101 Business Ideas – High Potential Businesses for the 21st Century

Looking to launch a successful business in today's world? 101 Business Ideas – High Potential Businesses for the 21st Century is your ultimate guide to turning inspiration into enterprise. This comprehensive book unveils 101 innovative business ventures across various industries.

MARKETING Summarized
Master the Art of Branding, Digital Strategies, and Customer Engagement in the Modern Era

Step into the dynamic world of marketing like never before! This isn't just another textbook—it's your ultimate guide to mastering the strategies, tools, and innovations that drive today's most successful brands. Unlock your potential.

ENTREPRENEURSHIP Summarized
The Complete Guide to Starting, Growing, and Scaling a Successful Business

This is not just another book about entrepreneurship—it's your blueprint for building something extraordinary, for breaking free from the ordinary, and for redefining what's possible. Are you ready to take the leap?

PRODUCT DEVELOPMENT Summarized
A Comprehensive Guide to Creating, Launching, and Managing Market-Winning Products

Every groundbreaking product starts with a spark—but only those who master the journey from idea to market truly succeed. Are you ready to join their ranks? [...] This book will give you the edge you need to succeed in a fast-moving, competitive world. Don't just develop products—shape the future.

SUPPLY CHAIN Summarized
A Comprehensive Guide to Strategies, Analytics, and Innovations for Efficient, Resilient, and Sustainable Supply Chains

In a world where supply chains power every industry—from the gadgets in your hand to the food on your table—mastering the art and science behind them has never been more critical. Are you ready to transform challenges into opportunities and lead in the age of interconnected global commerce?

PRODUCTION Summarized
A Comprehensive Guide to Efficient Manufacturing, Lean Systems, and Sustainable Production for Business Success

A Comprehensive Guide to Efficient Manufacturing, Lean Systems, and Sustainable Production for Business Success [...] your blueprint for success. Your journey to production mastery begins here. Let's build something extraordinary.

OPERATION MANAGEMENT Summarized
Master the Fundamentals of Operations, Supply Chains, and Process Optimization for Business Success

Unlock the secrets to operational excellence and take your business to new heights! In today's fast-paced, hyper-competitive world, mastering Operation Management isn't just a skill—it's a necessity. Dive in today and lead your business to operational success!

MANAGEMENT Summarized
A Comprehensive Guide to Mastering Leadership, Strategy, and Organizational Success

Unlock the Secrets to Mastering Leadership, Strategy, and Organizational Success. If you're ready to step into your full potential, lead with confidence, and create lasting impact, this is the book for you. Transform your career. Transform your world.

PROJECT MANAGEMENT Summarized
The Ultimate Guide to Mastering Agile, Risk, and Resource Strategies for Successful Projects

In the fast-paced world of business and innovation, project management is the superpower that transforms ideas into reality.

Don't just manage projects—own them. Step into the driver's seat of your career, empowered with strategies that turn challenges into opportunities.

COMPETITION Summarized
Master the Fundamentals, Strategies, and Future Trends to Dominate Competitive Markets

In a world where every decision can mean the difference between triumph and failure, competition reigns supreme. From boardrooms to battlefields, from bustling markets to global megacorporations, competition drives progress, fuels innovation, and shapes the future of industries and societies.

HUMAN RESOURCES Summarized
A Comprehensive Guide to HR Strategies, Practices, and Trends for Success in the Modern Workplace

Unlock the secrets to mastering the art and science of managing people in today's dynamic business world. Perfect for professionals and newcomers alike, this is the one book your career — and your organization — cannot afford to miss. The future of HR is here. Are you ready to lead it?

Psychology Summit Collection

Unlock the secrets of the mind and drive your personal growth to new heights with the Psychology Summit Collection – a comprehensive library of psychology wisdom. This series brings together holistic analyses of psychology, cognitive science, and human behavior with concise reference guides, giving you the ultimate toolkit for understanding the mind and applying its lessons in everyday life. Whether you're a psychology enthusiast, a business professional, a student, or on a self-improvement journey, this collection will elevate your knowledge and empower you to influence behavior and achieve lasting change.

Start your ascent with the Psychology Summit Collection today – and become the master of your mind.

101 Psychology Ideas - Understand the Mind, Influence Behavior, and Achieve Lasting Change

What if you could crack the code of the human mind and use it to improve every aspect of your life? 101 Psychology Ideas is your ultimate field guide to understanding how minds work and applying psychology to influence behavior and spark positive change. Take the first step toward lasting change and empowerment.

FAMILY PSYCHOLOGY Summarized
The Ultimate Guide to Family Dynamics, Parenting, Relationships, and Mental Health—Insights for Stronger Bonds and Lasting Happiness

What makes a family thrive? Why do some relationships deepen over time while others fracture under pressure? How can you foster resilience, love, and emotional intelligence in your household?

MOTHER AND CHILD PSYCHOLOGY Summarized
The Science of Maternal Bonding, Child Development, and Parenting Strategies for Lifelong Emotional and Cognitive Growth

What makes a mother's love so powerful? How does early bonding influence a child's intelligence, resilience, and sense of self? Why do some children thrive while others struggle emotionally? Unlock the Science of Mother-Child Bonding

FATHER AND CHILD PSYCHOLOGY Summarized
The Essential Guide to Parenting, Attachment, and Child Development for Stronger Father-Child Bonds

What does it truly mean to be a father? How does a man shape the mind, heart, and future of his child? Drawing from the latest psychological research and timeless wisdom, this book delves into the essential role of fathers—from the earliest days of infancy to adulthood. Fatherhood is not just a role—it is a legacy. Start building yours today.

SOCIAL PSYCHOLOGY Summarized
The Ultimate Guide to Human Behavior, Influence, and Decision-Making – Master Social Dynamics, Persuasion, and Psychological Triggers

What if you could decode every social interaction with scientific precision? What if you could persuade, influence, and connect with people effortlessly—whether in business, relationships, or everyday life? Are you ready to unlock the psychology of influence, persuasion, and social dynamics?

COGNITION Summarized
The Ultimate Guide to Understanding the Mind: Theories, Processes, and Practical Applications of Cognitive Science

What if you could unlock the mysteries of your own mind? What if you could master the art of thinking, decision-making, learning, and creativity like never before? Unlock the secrets of cognition. Transform the way you think. Buy your copy today.

PERCEPTION Summarized
A Comprehensive Guide to Understanding Human Perception: How We See, Hear, Feel, and Interpret Reality Across Senses, Cultures, and Technologies

What if everything you see, hear, and feel isn't what it seems? Rich with insights into vision, hearing, taste, touch, memory, and more, this book doesn't just explain perception—it shows you why it matters. Uncover how perception defines your reality.

PERSONALITY Summarized
A Comprehensive Guide to Traits, Theories, and Self-Discovery for Personal Growth and Success

Unlock the Secrets of Who You Are and Who You Can Become. What truly defines you? Are you born with your personality, or does the world shape it? Can you change who you are—or are you destined to remain the same? Are you ready to take control of your personality—and your destiny? Start your journey today.

BEHAVIOURAL PSYCHOLOGY Summarized
The Ultimate Guide to Understanding Human Behavior, Conditioning, and Behavior Modification Techniques

Unlock the Secrets of Human Behavior and Take Control of Your Life! Why do people act the way they do? How can habits be broken, behaviors reshaped, and decisions influenced? Prepare to see the world differently. And more importantly—learn how to change it.

DEVELOPMENTAL PSYCHOLOGY Summarized
Essential Guide to Human Growth, Behavior, and Lifespan Development – Key Theories, Research, and Practical Insights

Unlock the Secrets of Human Development – From Birth to Beyond! Why do we think, feel, and grow the way we do? How do childhood experiences shape our future? What drives personality, intelligence, and emotions across the lifespan? Are you ready to decode the blueprint of human development? Start your journey today!

Printed in Great Britain
by Amazon